# INCREDIBLE INDIA 2.0

Also by the same author:

*The Path Ahead: Transformative Ideas for India*

# INCREDIBLE INDIA 2.0

## SYNERGIES FOR GROWTH AND GOVERNANCE

AMITABH KANT

RUPA

Published by
Rupa Publications India Pvt. Ltd 2019
7/16, Ansari Road, Daryaganj
New Delhi 110002

*Sales centres:*
Bengaluru Chennai
Hyderabad Jaipur Kathmandu
Kolkata Mumbai Prayagraj



P-ISBN: 978-93-5333-730-8
E-ISBN: 978-93-5333-731-5

Fifth impression 2024

10 9 8 7 6 5



Printed in India

# Contents

## TWO
## BUSINESS AND ECONOMY

## THREE
## SOCIAL TRANSFORMATION



## FOUR
## INFRASTRUCTURE

## FIVE
## JUDICIARY

# Introduction

## India's Journey: From Lower-Middle Income to Upper-Middle Income

Since the economic reforms of the early 90s, India has made undeniable progress. We have pulled millions out of poverty and created one of the largest middle-class populations in the world. In current prices, India has overtaken France to become the sixth largest economy in the world and will soon surpass the United Kingdom as the fifth largest economy in the world.

However, this is not to say that our work is complete. In per capita terms, we fall towards the lower-middle income distribution. In purchasing power parity terms, our per capita income stands at $6,430, whilst that of China is $15,308. What is remarkable about China's growth story is that, in 1990, China's gross domestic product (GDP) per capita stood at $1,526, whereas India's stood at $1,754. Through sustained economic growth, China's per capita income now stands at 2.5 times that of India's. Clearly, growth is the only sustainable solution towards raising per capita incomes and standards of living.

The goal in front of India is clear—we need to transition towards a $5 trillion dollar economy, taking us from lower middle income status to upper middle income. We need to evolve into a highly competitive, efficient economy with social equity. The path of this transition is to be paved with reforms.

Competitiveness is determined at both the micro- and the macroeconomic level. Macroeconomic factors involve monetary and fiscal policy, human development and public institutions. Microeconomic competitiveness is a function of the business environment, regional development and sophistication of company operations. India needs to further develop its competitiveness at both the macro and micro level to lead this transition.

One cannot talk of transforming India without transforming the agriculture sector first. We need to move from agriculture to robust agri-business systems, whilst maintaining our food security, and critically, income security for farmers. Productivity needs to be enhanced, and at the same time, we need to ensure input use efficiency to lower costs of production.

Developing aggregation centres, packhouses and markets close to the farmgate in partnership with the private sector is the way forward. Gradually, we need to move towards a unified, real-time national market for farmers, enabling them to get the best price for their produce. States will have to take the lead in this aspect by instituting marketing reforms and land reforms to increase the average size of landholding.

We also need to reduce the dependency of our population on agriculture as a source of livelihood. According to most estimates, nearly 43 per cent of our labour force is involved in agriculture. This number needs to be brought down to global best practices. Manufacturing will play an important role in this regard. Export-led growth in this sector is what we need to target, particularly in labour-intensive sectors However, in order to capture larger shares of export markets, we must ensure that our firms are globally competitive. Rationalizing electricity tariffs, labour and land laws are critical enablers of firm competitiveness.

Industries of the future, colloquially known as Industry 4.0, need to be mainstreamed in India. Application of artificial intelligence (AI), blockchain and the Internet of Things (IoT) will be the key drivers of India's transition. Adoption of these new technologies is heavily dependent on an environment of innovation and entrepreneurship. The Atal Innovation Mission (AIM) is playing an important role in bringing innovation and entrepreneurship to the forefront through tinkering labs, incubation centres and grand challenges.

Infrastructure is another enabler of competitiveness. Several transformative steps have been taken in roads, airports, waterways and ports sectors. The pace of road construction for both highways and rural roads has picked up significantly, benefitting crores of people in the process. However, India needs to improve the regional distribution of this infrastructure. The Northeast region, for instance, lacks proper connectivity through road, rail or air, when compared to other parts of the country. Similarly, inland waterways remain untapped. More freight travels by road than rail, raising transportation costs. There is ample scope to increase investments in this sector, giving a huge fillip to the construction sector, which will, in turn, generate a large number of jobs, further absorbing the labour exiting agriculture.

The economic centre of gravity is increasingly shifting towards cities. According to Michael Porter, regions tend to be the most important economic unit for competitiveness. We must also create economic strategies around these cities and regions to address the regional disparities in India's growth story. By 2030, more than 600 million Indians will live in cities. Cities are drivers of growth, innovation and job creation. Innovation, job creation and sustainable urbanization hold the key to India's future. We must, therefore, use technology to recycle our water, convert our waste into energy and embed our cities with public transportation.

The Aspirational District Programme is a giant leap towards transforming India. It identified 115 of the most backward districts of India and makes them compete on a real-time basis on 49 indicators cutting across education, health, nutrition, skill development, infrastructure and agriculture. These are districts with extremely difficult geography, poor morale, lack of adequate doctors and teachers and virtually no monitoring. The programme ranks districts with the objective of making them the best performing district of their state within three years and amongst the best performing districts of India in five years' time. Monitoring and ranking, based on real-time grass-roots data, has led to a huge competitive spirit and spurred transformation on ground.

Opening up the coal sector for commercial mining, along with enhancing domestic oil and gas production and exploration, will also go a long way towards reducing India's dependence on the import of fossil fuels. In allocating these blocks, the focus should be on production, rather than revenue maximization. India must also continue its thrust towards renewable energy, especially in the area of storage and batteries. Breakthroughs in this area are likely to aid India in popularizing electric mobility as well.

Closely related to the competitiveness of regions is the future of mobility. India needs to drive a revolution in mobility, particularly shared mobility. With economic gravity shifting towards urban areas, shared mobility will be the key. This is to be achieved through shifting away from internal combustion engines to electric vehicles, especially in the case of two-wheelers, three-wheelers and buses. Creating this ecosystem of shared mobility will be a critical enabler of growth in urban areas. This is a sunrise area and India must create size and scale to become a global manufacturer of electric vehicles and batteries.

The connection between social and economic development is symbiotic. Improving India's competitiveness would require improvements on both parameters concurrently. This implies that investments in health, nutrition and education need to be ramped up significantly. For example, India spends approximately 1.4 per cent of its GDP on health services, whilst most upper-middle income countries spend close to 4 per cent.

Nutritional, health and educational outcomes need to be brought to the forefront. We will not be able to achieve growth rates of 9 to 10 per cent without transforming our human capital. For instance, the labour moving out of agriculture will have to be provided with skills to transition them into the manufacturing, construction or even service industries. Similarly, we must ensure that our new graduates are well-versed in the technologies and industries of the future.

Competitiveness is developed at both the macroeconomic level and the microeconomic level. In recent years, India has regained much of the macroeconomic competitiveness by stabilizing inflation, current account deficit and fiscal deficit. Investments in human capital is the other pillar of macroeconomic competitiveness, where investments have been ramped up. The business environment in India has become more conducive, judging by our improvement in ease of doing business. The agenda going forward should be on developing firm-level competitiveness and developing clusters that enable productivity and innovation.

There remain a host of challenges in front of India in its march towards an upper-middle income country. However, this does not mean that these challenges are insurmountable. All of us will have to work together—be it the government, civil society or private sector, in order to realize our collective ambitions for India. Growth has to come before redistribution.

In this publication, I have narrowed down the focus areas to what I consider to be the pillars of a world-beating nation. These are the developments in business and the economy towards making India the global hub for doing business, along with the efforts towards frontier technologies; governance reforms that enhance transparency, accountability, efficiency and ease of living; social sector development whether through an unprecedented exercise such as the Aspirational Districts Programme, Ayushman Bharat and the reform of the healthcare sector, reforms in education, and other social sector initiatives; and, reducing real-time challenges that we as a nation face and must address as soon as possible, whether it is the issue of pendency or challenges to the economy from judicial decisions, or managing the water crisis.

I have attempted to cover a vast range of aspects that will ensure that a rebranded India will be an India driving transformation and growth. Our potential is immense. We are the youngest nation, one filled with outstanding talent, quantitative skills and entrepreneurial zeal. Our focus on making India the global investment destination and our jump by 65 positions in the Ease of Doing Business rankings shows the introduction and rollout of the landmark goods and services tax (GST) regime and the Insolvency and Bankruptcy Code demonstrates the commitment of India towards becoming easy, simple and market-friendly. Strides in healthcare under the world's largest health insurance scheme, the National Nutrition Mission, and Swachh Bharat, are taking quality-of-life improvements to the remotest of villages and districts. Governance reforms such as direct benefit transfers (DBTs), Aadhaar-enabled welfare schemes, digitizing all processes and bringing in accountability have made life convenient and simpler for all of us.

I must also point out the gravity of the challenges that we must address immediately. Pendency of court cases and enforceability of contracts are critical challenges. Water management and the need to resolve the water crisis is another challenge that must be addressed immediately, through collaborative citizen-centric measures at the village, district, state and central level, with private sector engagement to ensure that water, our most precious commodity, does not remain scarce. Radically improving our nutritional standards and improving learning and health outcomes hold the key to our sustained growth. Similarly, we must endeavor to move towards a plastic-free society, and move from waste to wealth through effective recycling and waste management. The Prime Minister has brought the issue of water and making India single-use plastic-free centre stage, by constituting the Jal Shakti Ministry, launching the Jal Shakti Abhiyan and driving a mass movement against single-use plastic.

India is a nation on the move, and all of us should be proud of all that we have achieved. We must, however, not lose sight of the issues that must be addressed and resolved to ensure that there is no digression from an upward trajectory that we as a nation have chosen to follow. *Incredible India 2.0* will set a context of what we can expect by being a lighthouse nation that is visionary and progressive.

ONE

# GOVERNANCE

# Lateral Induction and Cross-Mobility Will Bring a Fresh Perspective

Reforms and development in a rapidly evolving and growing economy brings with it specific complexities and requirements for additional thought leadership at the policy and implementation stages, both on a state-wide basis as well as at the centre. This is why the recent announcement by the Government of India declaring the opening of ten positions at the joint secretary (JS) level as lateral entries is timely and necessary. India has a huge talent pool, laden with intellectual capital that outpaces any other country in the world. Unfortunately, at the policy and ministerial level, utilization of the best and brightest has not been enabled at an institutional level. All of that is set to change now. From the time I joined service, there were lateral inductions of sector leaders such as Shri Montek Ahluwalia, Shri Vijay Kelkar, Shri R.V Shahi and others. So, while it is not the first time that lateral entries have been attempted, it is certainly the first time that a group of 10 at the JS level is being inducted, out of the 450-plus JS-level positions in the government.

The process must be transparent, objective and entirely

merit-based. This is critical as the first step towards a broad-based institutionalization of a wider and deeper talent pool focusing on specific skill sets that fill the existing absence of talent in the government, tailored to the particular sector and enhanced by the industry-specific work experience that the lateral entry admissions will possess. It is also an opportunity to attract and retain the best and brightest from across the world that have a sector perspective and boost the ministry or department's capabilities and proficiency. The Union Public Service Commission (UPSC) is time-tested and selects the brightest individuals with immense and irreplaceable levels of field experience. Those coming through the UPSC have unique field experiences and comprehend the grass-roots challenges well. Civil servants, together with fresh inputs from lateral entrants, can provide synergies to policy and implementation like never before. The role of civil servants becomes even more vital, because for lateral inductions to get immersed in the government system will entail a steep learning curve. Significant hand-holding by the secretaries will be required to make the process effective. Possibly, a three-month induction and orientation course at the Lal Bahadur Shastri Academy may be considered.

## LEADING EXAMPLES

There are currently two outstanding examples at the secretary level of former bureaucrats with industry experience who are in critically important areas, and are excelling. Shri Parameswaran Iyer returned from a position with the World Bank to head the SBM as the secretary of the Ministry of Drinking Water and Sanitation. Similarly, Shri Indu Bhushan, a former bureaucrat and senior official at the Asian Development Bank, was recently appointed as CEO of the landmark Ayushman Bharat Yojana.

## SYNERGIES AND CROSS-MOBILITY

It is also imperative to allow civil servants and government officials to be placed in the private sector for periods of three to five years at a time. While the UPSC produces outstanding individuals, to make these individuals truly well-rounded, they should have the option to gain experience and specializations through private-sector placements. Cross-mobility will provide the ultimate synergy. For example, an individual who chose to be an academic, scientist, economist or entrepreneur, and didn't take the UPSC exam, but now wants to join the Government of India, should be allowed to be inducted laterally in the private sector.

## THE NITI AAYOG EXPERIENCE

Disruption is taking place in many sectors, and NITI Aayog has used the skill of industry professionals to great effect—complementary skills and congenial competition are the key aspects. If anything, by bringing in industry experience, it helps create a precedent and template for specializations, and placement in areas of interest and aptitude. For example, AIM is headed by a lateral seasoned professional with decades of industry experience in a leading technology consultancy, along with a team of young laterals, each with industry experience. AIM is today the catalyst for innovation, entrepreneurship and galvanizing the youth for a dynamic tomorrow.

Overall, NITI has a wide array of lateral representation,

in areas as diverse as education, health, AI, economics, agriculture, data analytics, law, energy, transport, sports and other growth sectors. This is in many ways the first step towards transforming India.

## THE WAY FORWARD

India is on track to achieve efficiencies and excellence to bring itself up to speed with the rest of the world. Lateral inductions are just one of the many steps taken by the Government of India in governance reforms that include outcome-based monitoring, ease of doing business and digital technology reforms.

Lateral inductions and cross-mobility will bring in a fresh perspective and cutting-edge ideas across both sectors as each avails the synergies created. The best and brightest talent must be allowed to bring vibrancy, expertise and perspective to make India a leader in intellectual human capital. This forward-thinking move by the government sets the ball rolling towards a congenial competition based on merit on both on the private and public side. A free flow of exposure and opportunity will be the difference in integrating progressive reform across the board, as India motors towards a New India in 2022.

# India's Quiet Administrative Reforms

It is not feasible for India to progress in the twenty-first century with nineteenth-century administrative systems. The idea of reforming India's vast and unwieldy administrative mechanism has been in the public discourse since the 60s. There have been two administrative reforms commissions four decades apart in 1996 and 2005. Both the commissions had submitted voluminous reports with vast number of recommendations, the majority of which remain unimplemented till date.

However, in the last three years, several innovative measures have been launched, which signal the government's intent to administratively leapfrog and make the administrative machinery far more efficient, decisive and cohesive. These include outcome-based monitoring of schemes, fast-tracking of projects at the highest level, creating a sense of competition across states and cities and ranking them, breaking silos between ministries, and inducting talent laterally in the government.

The first key reform is the shift in administrative focus from inputs and outputs to outcomes that are reviewed and monitored by the prime minister personally. Outcomes are what matter to citizens, not processes, procedures, formation of committees, etc. With focus on creating a citizen-centric and participatory model of governance, moving to an outcome-based system is a natural first step. Outcomes have been identified to track the right metrics for key sectors and formulate solutions for major challenges. Cross-dimensional outcomes have been deployed, for example, capacity, mobility, quality and safety have been identified as key outcome dimensions for road projects. In the case of railways, the key outcome is operating ratio, passenger and freight yields, capital spending, redevelopment of railway stations, and safety measures. For the first time, an outcome-based budget prepared by NITI Aayog was presented to the Parliament along with the main budget.

Sophisticated dashboards have been created for the regular monitoring of projects and periodic updates. Meeting minutes along with clear ownership and implementation timelines are released, and followed up periodically. Outcome-based reviews have a broad sweep—15 infrastructure and social sectors have been reviewed, covering 72 per cent of total budget outlay. Key decisions have also been taken post review; for example, it was decided to increase the modal share of railways from 33 per cent to 35 per cent in FY17, in line with the long-term goal of 50 per cent by 2032. Institutional reforms, such as in Medical Council of India (MCI), have also come up for review. The committee has since considered sweeping changes, proposing the creation of a National Medical Commission to replace MCI, ending a long era of inspection raj and ushering in major reforms to medical education.

The second key initiative, PRAGATI (Pro-Active Governance and Timely Implementation), is an initiative where key infrastructure and social sector projects that are facing implementation bottlenecks or are delayed, are being taken up for discussion and review at the prime minister's level. This involves video conferencing of all key stakeholders including representatives of central and state agencies. PRAGATI has several noteworthy features—it provides a forum for all stakeholders of key projects to voice their views and resolve issues, assigns clear responsibilities to officials along with strict timelines for implementation, expedites developmental projects by bringing the centre and states on the same platform, and brings key projects under close supervision of the highest officials in the country. It is also a means to break walls between different government agencies and enable sharing of the best practices. Before PRAGATI's meeting, issues are discussed and uploaded on a portal, statuses of projects are updated online and minutes of the meeting are put out for public display. Since its launch, 18 PRAGATI meetings have been held and state projects worth over ₹8.31 lakh crore across critical infrastructure sectors like railways, national highways, power, coal, civil aviation,etc., interminably delayed for the past several years, have been fast-tracked. The initiative has helped fast-track projects across states. Besides projects, 38 flagship programmes/schemes and grievances of 16 ministries/departments have also been reviewed. For instance, the Nangal Dam Talwara railway line, which had been pending since 1981, has been put on fast-track. Other projects like Salma Dam in Afghanistan, the rail-cum-road bridge over Ganga in Patna, and Aadhaar enrolment by the UIDAI and the Registrar General of India have moved rapidly forward post PRAGATI intervention. In many ways, PRAGATI has been a unique mechanism. It brought stakeholders together, broke open walls between the centre and the state, shifted focus to outcomes and deadlines, and created a transparent dashboard to monitor implementation. This has made a radical difference to implementation on ground.

The third major administrative reform has been the creation of an immense sense of competitive spirit amongst states and districts by ranking them and increasingly selecting them for projects through a challenge method. The Ease of Doing Business index ranking of states has led states to initiate radical reforms by eliminating a vast number of rules, regulations and procedures. Competitive pressure has led to newer states like Telangana, Jharkand and Chhattisgarh, making a quantum jump forward. The ranking of districts in terms of cleanliness under the Swachh Bharat initiative has also had a major impact and has spurred change at the municipal level. The selection of cities for the Smart City Programme through a challenge methodology has led cities to undertake reforms in urbanization and projects by forming Special Purpose Vehicles (SPVs) and housing all approvals in the SPVs.

The fourth key reform has been the formation of groups of secretaries to break silos, stimulate thinking that can cut across ministries, and develop a roadmap for growth with commitment of all stakeholders. Eight groups of secretaries were constituted to work on themes ranging from 'Accelerated Growth with Inclusion and Equity' to 'Employment Generation Strategies' and 'Energy Conservation and Efficiency'. These groups were supported by similar groups of JSs. An innovative aspect of these groups was that it involved senior officials whose departments were not directly related to the theme. This encouraged cross-sector thinking and the generation of creative ideas. The exercise has been continued this year with greater vigour and energy, and groups have been tasked to pursue and get their final recommendations implemented.

Reforms are not possible if mindsets don't change. Several initiatives have been formulated to bring in new thinking and innovative ideas. Doing away with resource allocation-focused Planning Commission, scrapping of 1,175 obsolete laws and merging of railways and union budget are all steps to make India an easier and simpler place to do business in and to enhance the quality of governance. Measures like scrapping the distinction between planned and non-planned expenditures in annual budget will also help shift focus from reducing revenue deficit to increasing capital spending, setting in motion the process for improvement in fiscal deficit quality. Lateral entry has been instituted at senior levels at NITI Aayog. At NITI Aayog, it was the young professionals who primarily shouldered the task of explaining the different modes of digital payments across central ministries and states via digi-dhan melas when demonetization was introduced. Secondments have also been introduced so that talented individuals from the private sector with passion to effect meaningful change through the government, could do so while keeping their career path intact. These are all path-breaking measures.

While it may take time for these reforms to manifest fully, the direction is right and the pace is brisk. Administrative reforms will have to remain a continuous process but a lot has been achieved quietly in the last three years.

# NITI Aayog as an Agent of India's Transformation

NITI Aayog, established in 2015, is one of Indian democracy's youngest institutions. Established with the mandate of reimagining the development agenda by dismantling old-style central planning, it was mandated to foster cooperative federalism, evolve a national consensus on developmental goals, redefine the reforms agenda, act as a platform for resolution of cross-sectoral issues between centre and state governments, capacity-building, and act as a knowledge and innovation hub—a massive mandate for a nascent organization.

The completion of three years of its existence offers an opportunity to introspect on whether NITI enabled transformation to a New India or was it the same entity in a different garb. In my personal opinion, NITI did live up to its name and bring about a transformational change in the manner policymaking is practised and perceived in this country.

First, cooperative and competitive federalism has been firmly entrenched by NITI in the planning landscape of the country. Major policy processes have been preceded by consultation in different fora. Recommendations on rationalization of centrally sponsored schemes, skill development, Swachh Bharat Mission, agriculture development and digital payments were all debated in committees having state governments. Based on their recommendations, The Central Secretarial Service have been rationalized into 28 umbrella schemes, several initiatives have been taken to promote digital payments, and other recommendations are being implemented.

Innovative schemes, premised on centre-state partnership, were launched viz. Sustainable Action for Transforming Human Capital (SATH), aimed at initiating transformation in education and health sectors by hand-holding states; developing Support Services to States (DSSS) for development of infrastructure; promoting public-private partnership (PPP) in district hospital in Tier II/Tier III for treatment of select non-communicable processes; transformation of 115 identified aspirational districts through focus on technology and sharing of best practices; and Ek Bharat Shrestha Bharat (EBSB) to make the country united, strong and promote excellence in all walks of life through long-term interstate engagements in cultural exchanges and education.

To nurture a sense of competition amongst the states where they compete with each other to avail benefits under specific schemes, a unique challenge method was evolved, which was in stark contrast to allocation of funds by the erstwhile Planning Commission. Performance and ranking of states in critical sectors with emphasis on outcomes, like health, education, water and digital transformation, was done to nudge them into competing with each other for better results, practices and innovations.

In addition, states were assisted in critical areas like development of Human Development Report, regulatory reform through consolidation of laws and resolution of pending issues of states with central ministries.

Keeping with its mandate to enhance productive efficiency, NITI enabled the strengthening of public sector enterprises' performances through enabling strategic disinvestment of more than 30 Central Public Sector Enterprises (CPSEs) till date, including Air India where there was a long gap of 14 years and closure of more than 15 sick/loss-making/non-performing CPSEs.

Towards balanced regional development, NITI provided the roadmap for a new industrial policy for Northeastern and Himalayan states, undertook a unique exercise of holistic and sustainable development of 10 islands, constituted an Island Development Agency (IDA) under the union home minister and enabled Geographic Information System (GIS)-based planning in all the states and union territories (UTs).

Health and agriculture are the two sectors where NITI has enabled path-breaking changes in a stark contrast of past planning processes. Medical Council of India Bill, prepared by NITI, which is in the Parliament, would usher in a new era of medical education and break the stranglehold of the corrupt MCI. National Nutrition Strategy formulated by NITI and the setting up of the National Nutrition Mission will enable targeted drive at tackling malnutrition that has plagued the children of this country. Agriculture sector that had failed to experience transformational reforms previously witnessed transformational reforms in land tenancy and administration, agricultural marketing, etc.

Following the paradigm shift from outlays to outcome-based governance and towards improving efficacy of government schemes, NITI undertook an ambitious initiative of institutionalizing monitoring outcomes of such schemes. The development, monitoring and evaluation office in NITI was set up with the task of programme and sectoral monitoring and evaluation using a web-based interactive dashboard. Rigorous exercise to bring qualitative improvement in the output-outcome framework in the union budget by reviewing and identifying relevant outputs and outcomes, quantifiable and measurable indicators, and monitoring them will transform the budget process.

To promote stakeholder consultation and enable expert advice in policymaking, unique initiatives were launched, like 'SAMAVESH', wherein 34 knowledge and research institutions have signed a memorandum of understanding with NITI for knowledge sharing and linking policy with practice; NITI Lecture series where global thought leaders address top policymakers on varied topics to instil debate and catalyze fresh thought in governance; and Champions of Change where young CEOs and entrepreneurs made policy prescriptions.

Seminal publications like the compendium on the states' best practices across all sectors, titled *States Forward: Best Practices from Our States* and *Good Practices Resource Book* (2015) to consolidate the innovative good practices in social security, infrastructure, child protection and local governance; real-time knowledge portal to share the best practices across sectors and the states, which is to be shortly launched; and India Energy Portal are a few initiatives that enabled NITI to become a state-of-the-art resource centre for research on good governance and best practices.

NITI has brought in a major change in promoting an entrepreneurial ecosystem. Under its much acclaimed AIM, NITI has supported Atal Tinkering Labs (ATLs) in schools to foster creativity and scientific temper in students and Atal Incubation Centres to help start-ups expand quicker and enable innovation-entrepreneurship in core sectors such as manufacturing, transport, energy, education, agriculture, water and sanitation.

Successful hosting of the Global Entrepreneurship Summit 2017 by NITI won much global acclaim for the country and firmly placed it on the global entrepreneurial map. To maintain the momentum, it is proposed to set up a women entrepreneurship cell.

NITI is integrally engaged in promotion and supporting the adoption of frontier technology. The drive to promote digital payments post-demonetization saw great success using many innovative initiatives. Spearheading the shared, connected and clean mobility solutions to be adopted in smart cities, NITI published reports and a pilot on the proposal to develop electric vehicle infrastructure in Delhi-NCR from Noida to Gurgaon. Adoption of AI and blockchain technologies in various sectors for good governance is actively pursued. A unique initiative of setting up a national data and analytics portal is also on the anvil that besides being a single-point source of sectoral data for researchers, policymakers and citizens, will also enable training sharing data sets between different organizations for AI applications.

Thus, through its various endeavours, NITI has not merely lived up to its name, but provided energy, vitality and dynamism to the process of transforming India. It aims to fulfil the aspirations of its population, adopt the latest technology to improve the lives and well-being of its populace, and strives towards a sustainable development.

# The Technological Leapfrog of Governance: How Technology is Driving Efficiency and Effectiveness in Government

During my tenure in Kerala I got a unique opportunity to work in the fisheries sector of Kerala. The task was to improve the livelihood of traditional fishermen. The sector was riddled with middlemen and the fishermen were getting only 25 per cent of the market price for fish. We formed self-help groups and provided them with new technology—fibreglass crafts, outboard motors and fishing nets—to enhance their production and productivity. We also introduced beach-level auctions so that the earnings from daily catch could be deposited in their bank accounts. The biggest challenge we faced was to get bank accounts opened for the fishermen. It took us 10 months of chasing physical banks and bank managers to get this done. The process of 'Know Your Customer' was a nightmare. Contrast this with my experience last month. I walked into a bank branch and opened my account using my biometric on a handheld device in one minute flat. From 10 months to one minute has been the paradigm shift.

In the last few years, governance in India across sectors has been redefined through business process re-engineering, technology and data analytics. In coming years, India will see a new culture where decisions will be based on large sets of data, application of AI and machine learning to arrive at sound decisions. Digital technology is reshaping the way government is designing and implementing programmes. The use of technology has brought in better systems, greater efficiency and is beginning to have a profound impact on governance.

Let us analyse a few areas:

First, India has combined the used of unique biometric identifiers and financial inclusion for effectiveness in social benefits and to reduce the vast number of illegitimate beneficiaries under welfare programmes. DBT has been implemented across 437 schemes and has helped save ₹83,000 crore till date. Its implementation has led to 2.75 crore duplicate, fake or non-existent ration cards being deleted and 3.85 crore duplicate and inactive consumers for LPG subsidy being eliminated.

Second, the Public Financial Management System (PFMS) has led to the creation of a financial management platform for all plan schemes, a database of all recipient agencies, integration with the core banking solution of banks, integration of state treasurers and tracking of fund flow to the lowest tier of implementation of plan schemes on real-time basis. PFMS has also led to just-in-time release of funds and efficient management in use of funds, including ultimate utilization. This year on 28 March 2018, an amount of ₹72,000 crore has been digitally transacted through the PFMS portal for 98 lakh transactions. This is a historic record of digital transactions processed in a single day. NITI

Aayog has finalized a real-time monitoring dashboard that will for the first time give a comprehensive view of public spending versus performance on outcomes of all government expenditure.

Third, digitization has led to lower costs in the collection of direct taxes. Almost 98.5 per cent of all income tax returns have been filed online. The income tax department received 6.84 crore income tax returns in FY 17–18, a growth of 26 per cent and an additionality of more than one crore new tax returns.

Fourth, Unified Payment Interface (UPI) and Bharat Bill Payment System (BBPS) have triggered a plethora of private-sector innovated apps that have significantly eased citizens' bill payments towards services provided by the government. BBPS has more than doubled the number of bills paid digitally from April 2017, when the pilot was launched. The value of bills paid on the platform has jumped by about 46 per cent during this period. This demonstrates that the common citizen finds enormous ease in paying digitally. According to a KPMG report, the size of bill payments market in India is projected to reach ₹9.4 trillion by 2020.

Fifth, digital payment transactions have now become extremely simple, easy and convenient, thanks to Bhim UPI. We have seen the emergence of Google Pay and WhatsApp payment. During 2017–18, India has seen over a billion transactions in volume and over a trillion transactions in value. In the coming years, there will be increased disruption with new players and new technologies.

Finally, the rollout of GST has resulted in a 50 per cent increase in unique indirect taxpayers as compared to the pre-GST system. This translates to a substantial 3.4 million new indirect taxpayers leading to a radical formalization of the Indian economy.

A recent study predicts that digital transformation will add \$154 billion to India's GDP by 2021, increasing the growth rate by 1 per cent annually. In 2017, about 4 per cent of the country's GDP was derived from digital products and services created directly through the use of technologies like Cloud, IoT and AI. According to an analysis by Accenture, AI has the potential to add US\$957 billion, or 15 per cent of current gross value added, to India's economy in 2035. India offers challenges that can be solved by application of AI in areas that are vastly different from the Western world. We are attempting to find solutions in areas such as agriculture, healthcare and education.

NITI Aayog is working to implement AI solutions to improve crop productivity and soil health on farms by using remote sensing images and other data available with the government. It is also exploring the inception of a natural language processing platform that can provide AI applications to do natural language processing. NITI is also partnering medical institutions to build a 'bio bank'—radiological and pathological images.

The ambitious 'Modicare' Ayushman Bharat Scheme will link primary and community health centres with district hospitals. Apart from the ₹5,00,000 financial insurance which will cover 50 crore Indians, it will ensure provision of healthcare through a digital, paperless, cashless, portable scheme. The health stack linked to Aadhaar will be transformational.

Blockchain is fast becoming a new operating system for facilitating digital transactions across financial markets, supply chains and content ecosystems. Blockchain technologies offer solutions for India that can improve the ease of doing business, especially in the areas of enforcement of contracts and registering of property. It can potentially eliminate 40 lakh cases relating to land and land disputes. NITI is working on blockchain-based smart contracts which will reduce litigation and land registry on the blockchain, thus reducing corruption relating to land. It is estimated that 25 per cent of domestic medicines are fake. NITI's drug authenticity project will empower consumers to verify the genuineness of drugs sold as their manufacturing will be tracked on the blockchain. India has a billion biometrics on Aadhaar. We have a unique opportunity to leverage our public identities to have many applications on the blockchain architecture.

India has for years been a highly complex, complicated and difficult nation for its citizens with a vast number of forms, papers and procedures. This had made it extremely difficult for the common man to access government services. The rapid adoption of digital technology across sectors is making things increasingly simple and easy and eliminating all forms of human intervention. It has enabled India to jump up 42 positions in World Bank's Ease of Doing Business index. The adoption of AI, blockchain, data analytics and machine learning will provide greater impetus for achieving a major jump in the efficiency and effectiveness of governance.

# NewSpace Technologies for a New India

India's space odyssey began in the early 1960s with the launch of a sounding rocket (Nike-Apache) supplied by NASA. In this period, spanning about 60 years, India's credential as a space power has grown enormously and today we are amongst the top four countries in space exploration and capability. The indigenously designed and developed Indian Remote Sensing (IRS) and Indian National Satellite System (INSAT) satellites series have been operating in the entire Asia Pacific region, offering communications and imagery services in multiple resolutions, bands, and swaths to cater to a wide user base in India and in the neighbourhood. More recent success include the Chandrayaan-1, the Mangalyaan, IRNSS or NaViC programme, the ASAT capability development and significant design improvements in the launch vehicle and Earth-based processing analytics. We also set up the Indian Institute of Space Science and Technology about 12 years ago to develop the best possible HR base for this strategic sector.

However, we cannot rest on our laurels as the global space sector is undergoing rapid transformations as space-based applications have witnessed tectonic changes. What was once curiosity for scientists has become cash for business.

Due to the importance of the services that space-based systems provide for civil society and national security, new-use cases are being progressively innovated, disrupting the space economy as we know it.

In the security architecture of nation states, the US has the Air Force Space Command that is responsible for ensuring the friendly use of space as well as counter-space operations for those disturbing the order, and providing space-based services such as communications, navigation, weather prediction and intelligence to improve operations. India has established the Defence Space Agency and the Defence Space Research Organisation in the interest of national security.

With substantial and highly qualified access to space technology programmes, innovators and visionaries who are able to combine other disciplines in innovating new products and applications are constantly seeing the space business transforming at a pace that was unimaginable a few years ago. Elon Musk's SpaceX is a prime example. Who would have thought that one day, NASA would no longer launch US Government satellites into space? SpaceX reduced the launch cost to less than a fourth of NASA launches.

Jeff Bezos, under his Blue Origin programme, is introducing Reusable Launch Vehicles (RLVs) and visualizing offshoring production into space/moon to leverage the benefits of ZERO power cost. Interestingly, the concept was derived from Otis Elevator invention, which in some way is a reusable launch and recovery vehicle taking you from the ground to the $100^{th}$ floor repeatedly, and halting anywhere in between. That one innovation made it feasible to design high-rise buildings, minimizing ground footprint, compacting habitation and optimizing utility and support systems. The RLV is also likely to become our elevator to space, spawning innovative applications.

These space applications can be broadly classified into—Communications and Entertainment; Imagery and Analytics; and, Position Navigation and Timing Services. India has already achieved great success in the first two applications and with the commissioning of the IRNSS India, joins a select league of nations with their own space-based positioning and navigational systems. This segment becomes particularly pivotal to national security if a GNSS system is spoofed or denied to a user. It can be catastrophic for logistics and transportation, finance and many security systems.

In this milieu, we are seeing a stream of new players from all parts of the world entering the space sector and paving the way to the 'space economy'. In a sense, the world has already entered the NewSpace era—which I would like to call the Next Space so that subsequent improvements may be designated as 'New Space after Next' and then 'NextGen Space'—which, going by the rapidity with which business is adopting technology, may be not too far away. Several disruptive technologies and innovative business models are on the horizon and therefore 'more of the usual' incremental improvements may not be the approach to adopt for the NewSpace era. Adapting novel business models will be as important as adopting new technology.

Overarching elements driving innovation in the space sector are the key opportunities in national security and science objectives—the expansion of downstream space applications with new-use cases developing every day in the pursuit of exploration and exploitation of space.

Traditionally, a key source of innovation for the space sector were public-funded research and development through government-owned space agencies and laboratories pursuing identified and sponsored programmes with governmental funding, More recently, in particular in the US, new companies have entered the space sector—funded by venture capitalists and angel investors—introducing a new source of innovation based on new business models, disruptive technologies and the rigorous spinning-in of terrestrial technologies, mass production components and mass production methods from other mature terrestrial industries, which together are creating the 'New Space Economy'.

This shift in paradigm is further being enhanced by the entrance of commercial actors from the Internet economy into the space sector, which promotes, in addition, the stronger spinning-in of software and artificial intelligence techniques. Consequently, the rate of innovation in the sector has substantially increased and capital and operating costs in many areas have been brought down significantly.

The key technologies driving the business are newer and sustained Access to Space, opening of 5G communications technologies, higher resolution and revisit rates for Earth Observation, developing faster and more accurate Positioning Timing and Navigation, Space Exploration & Human Flight and Cybersecurity/Data Science.

Let's begin with access to space. This access was once limited to highly trained and qualified astronauts. But today, in the realm of space tourism, companies like Virgin Galactic and SpaceX are outlining plans to deliver various forms of commercial spaceflights in the near future. The key enabler is the replacement of expendable launch vehicles with reusable launch vehicles. Due to its potential for cost reductions, reusability will, in the long term, likely become a key determinant for the competitiveness of commercial launch providers.

The emergence of highly capable small satellite and small satellite constellations powered into space by small launch vehicles are showing a promising commercial potential. Upstream requirements would be to develop a new generation of space high-performance engines, capable of deep throttling for soft landings and controlling flight at variable speeds and altitudes and ultra-light and ultra-strong smart materials—better thermal protection for example. In the future as propulsion technologies advance, development of small launchers may also be helpful for low-cost testing of a variety of technologies needed for reusability, be it for small or heavy launchers.

A second area where the New Space economy is making rapid strides in is in the field of communications. Developing economies and remote areas in developed economies can often access the global information infrastructure only via satellites. Traditional telecommunications markets are based on geostationary satellites that are expected to remain fairly stable. However, new dynamics within the market are expected to be provided by low-flying small satellite constellations using hundreds or even thousands of satellites. OneWeb is building the 'world's first global communications network in space that will deliver high-throughput, high-speed services capable of connecting everywhere, to everyone...' These advances would require a different set of technologies including concepts for next-generation collaborative small satellite data telecom constellations, small-scale transmitters/receivers for optical inter-satellite links etc. and the world' first mass-produced satellite constellation network. Imagine what it could do to mobile telephony services as we know them—comprising towers, re-transmitters, leased line cables and related services.

When we speak of imagery and Earth Observation, a huge portfolio of passive and active sensors, spanning the optical, infrared and radar regions of the electromagnetic spectrum are already in operation. Smarter sensors such as LiDAR and I-SAR are in the offing. Hence the full potential of satellite-based earth observation has still not been unveiled. Nations and economies today are developing new-use cases for a variety of applications in security, services and industry. Earth Observation Satellites of ISRO have been successfully able to establish many operational applications in the country. Both at central and state level, there is a large number of users who utilize space-based inputs for various purposes and their numbers will only grow as better imagery and data interpretation technologies are developed.

In the maritime domain for example, space-based Synthetic Aperture Radars are able to detect ships and crafts that have 'gone silent' and have become dark vessels. The purpose can be to beat sanctions, engage in illegal fishing and poaching, illegal human immigration, carriage of drugs, narcotics and small arms and several other sinister businesses, all of which have a downstream impact on national security and the economy. Satellites are an important element of the Maritime Domain Awareness/Blue Economy ecosystem with its ability for Dark Vessel Detection, Oil Spill monitoring, Illegal Unreported and Unregulated (IUU) Fishing, iceberg monitoring, pollution and erosion of coastal regions etc. Combined with other technologies, satellite imagery can generate various options for voyage optimization by predicting weather and sea conditions en route, port congestion, security alerts of piracy and terrorism etc.

Apart from the security portfolio, there are numerous other use cases being promoted. The significant advances in defense and strategic space applications pale when compared to the commercial space sector that continues to grow and diversify at an unprecedented pace. Entrepreneurs with a wide range of backgrounds and companies of all sizes are developing new applications as new ideas potentially disrupt our thinking about uses of space. They employ legacy industrial concepts like standardization, reusability and continuous learning, whilst leveraging the potential of emerging technologies like cloud computing, advanced material and manufacturing, and artificial intelligence.

The farm and fishing sectors offer huge potential for Earth Observation and imagery by which satellites can monitor crop health and forecast crop yields with timely sub-meter imagery. They can not only detect but also identify pest infestation and plan irrigation levels to augment precision agriculture techniques. This would help predict crop yields and assist commodity traders in estimating market supplies, farm insurance agencies in settling claims etc. Soil moisture monitoring using satellite imagery can also provide an assessment of surface moisture conditions in real-time across the entire surface, rather than for a single point like ground-based soil moisture and weather sensors.

Irrigated agriculture is the principal consumer of freshwater resources. Most countries do not have a precise measurement of water consumption for irrigation. Remote sensing has been an effective tool to monitor irrigated lands in many locations around the world as their spectral responses are different from non-irrigated croplands. It is entirely possible to compare the water requirement for each crop and compare it with the water drawn by a farmer, thus devising better water-saving strategies and smart irrigation practices. Considering water and electricity is subsidized, its wanton utilization could be curtailed. Designing imagery solutions could lead to large-scale benefits through introducing use-based energy/water-dynamic water pricing, assist in crop selection and market intelligence and access, and open up the private sector procurement supply chain.

One of the key goals under Sustainable Development Goal 14 is to restore fish stocks to sustainable levels. Recently, the department of fisheries has released data on the national marine fish catch, which shows a decline in the catch and also identifies emerging asymmetries in fish stock by type and location. Satellites are using techniques to determine oceanographic, hydrological and nutrient analysis to locate potential fish zones. A reliable and timely advisory on the potential zones of fish aggregation will benefit the fishing community to reduce the time and effort spent in searching shoals of fish.

However, the continuing decline in global fish stocks places an increasing importance on remote surveillance of fishing vessel to enforce fishing regulations and counter IUU fishing activities. Satellite remote sensing systems can detect IUU fishing and high-resolution imagery can identify and possibly recognize the miscreants and their masters. Satellite synthetic aperture radar (SAR) systems are also able to detect offshore vessels and have the advantage of all-weather operations.

Earth Observation can also provide early warnings on refugee movements and infrastructure development in conflict areas to aid humanitarian efforts. Other new businesses emerging include insurance modeling through risk exposure models to make more informed commodity trading decisions.

High-frequency monitoring of oil and gas storage and pipeline monitoring for changes in volumes, pilferage and vegetation is another application that has already matured to some extent. The Mining sector is using various techniques to create digital elevation models—DEMs—to determine mining quantities and quality. These applications will require a large number of Small Satellites and combination of systems that can fuse data from space, air and terrestrial-based sensors, using multispectral/hyperspectral/SAR image processing to develop composite synthetic image of the area of interest.

Using satellite imagery to develop DEMs for water-starved or flood-prone areas can also provide predictive inputs for planners. Combined with legacy data imagery, it can identify potential routes to bunds and water bodies that can be opened up at minimum cost and time. Similarly, it would be possible to identify flooding zones depending upon simulating rainfall on a digitized topography of the region.

The ability of Global Navigation Satellite Systems (GNSS) to continue to improve accuracies in Position Navigation & Timing is becoming critical for a host of services not only for navigation but also for tracking and tracing of vehicles and cargo. Other examples include developing transparency in financial transactions, management of power plants and electrical grids and telecommunication networks. This sector is now attracting innovators and investors venturing into what was once a government preserve. Atomic clocks and system time generation embedded with integrity measures with resistance to interference and spoofing; interoperability between different GNSS platforms and systems and mitigating natural impairments (e.g. atmospheric delays, multipath of signals) and intentional disturbances such as jamming and spoofing are areas where innovators are engaged. Various systems such as China's BeiDou, EUs Galileo, Russia's GLONASS, India's NaViC, and Japan's QZSS are virtually competing in space for space.

Whilst the NewSpace economy is engaged in the benign pursuit of opportunities to improve the lot of humankind, regressive forces are also at work. Cybersecurity is a real and malignant threat to the use of space and its users. Satellites, satellite constellations and other parts of the space segment have always been IT-infrastructure intensive, for example in uplinking command and control instructions or downlinking the information from their sensors and payloads back to the terrestrial user. Vital infrastructures and services such as telecommunications, financial services, weather forecasting, and safety and security services heavily rely on these space-based systems and therefore these systems must be firewalled from potential disruptions.

Space security and cybersecurity, together referred to as 'cyberspace', constitute a unique technological domain that is becoming a prominent focus for international strategic, political, and economic competition. Such a disruption can have a very significant impact on the national economy and security. The currently implemented security safeguards in space-based systems and its operations will need to continuously evolve in order to remain ahead of the curve of the disruptors and hackers. At the geo-political level, nations need the capability to defend their own systems and defeat antagonistic systems. The ASAT test by India is a testimony to that capability.

Even as India has journeyed for close to sixty years in this domain, there are several strategies, both short term and long term, that may need to be developed by our scientists, strategists and policymakers to expand the utilization of space assets and increasing the overall size of the country's space economy. These include requirements that need to be addressed for India to maximize its gains and the potential of its strong capacity to build satellites and launch vehicles particularly for applications in agriculture, fishing and forestry, water management, urban planning, maritime domain surveillance, low-cost high-speed internet systems for 'assisted education' in rural areas, and remote consultancy for health services. Up to an extent, government funding and organized and structured R&D has taken us to where we have reached. But in the future, if we are to take note of the world elsewhere, it is entrepreneurs and innovators who are rapidly piercing the frontiers of NewSpace. We must also encourage the graduates from the Indian Institute of Space Science and Technology to seek entrepreneurial opportunities in the NewSpace economy. Of course, ISRO and the Government should support creating innovation hubs and incubation centres, appropriate test and trials facilities etc.

Whilst there are alternative views about the overall future of space, the impact that space plays in our daily lives today is a given. Going forward, the Indian space programme may need to become more inclusive and expansive by forging international space partnerships, both governmental and commercial, and developing models on how private business enterprise can participate in all aspects of the larger NewSpace value chain from conceptual design to components manufacturing and various space-based services. In the not-too-distant future we could see the use of reusable launch vehicles travelling to space to collect 'free' but highly valuable space debris for processing into new materials on earth. As the corridors of space get crowded with satellites, a suitable traffic management solution is an inescapable necessity.

In conclusion, the space narrative is rich in sources of inspiration and international cooperation but these engagements are also a story of the advancement of space technologies. Questions related to the history of the universe and the solar system, the origin of life and the possibilities of the extension of the human presence beyond Earth will continue to remain focal areas and the purpose of space exploration for scientists. For lesser mortals, progress in computational technologies and data analytics, miniaturization and robotics technologies, autonomous capabilities, newer materials and propulsion technologies will make space-derived applications more widespread and affordable. Costs for human spaceflight activities will be further brought down substantially by using low-cost launchers and reusable launch vehicles. For the Reusable Launch Vehicles and space habitation, the key technologies being developed include development of entry, descent and landing technologies as well as moon rover technologies, development of low-cost pressurized modules and habitats, bio-regenerative systems and many more. These are the avenues to the gates of the NewSpace economy.

However, there is a jungle out there with predators sensing potential kills in disrupting economies and security structures. So whilst we must tread this path with enthusiasm and energy to leave a better world for our next generations, we should also be careful and cautious that our programmes do not fall prey to space predators. Commensurate security architectures and resources must accompany the journey to the NewSpace economy.

# DRDO Spearheads Transformation

The DRDO has grown from its limited beginnings in 1958 with 10 laboratories and establishments, to a multidimensional and multifaceted agency of more than 50 establishments, 5000 scientists, 25,000 technicians and staff devoted to developing defence and aerospace technologies, and covering a variety of applications across aeronautics to armament and missiles to materials.

We frequently hear of the path-breaking contribution that our scientists at DRDO have made towards development of high-technology missiles, radars and sonars, weapons, vehicles and tanks, which makes India not only proud but also leads the country to the Make in India path of self-reliance.

We have also learnt that the DRDO has mentored a large number of start-ups and has been a source of incubation for young minds to develop innovative products using local technology and providing local solutions for local problems. More recently, the DRDO has taken highly positive and meaningful steps towards further encouraging research activities and developmental projects through the Technology Development Fund. It has opened its laboratories and test centres for use by the private sector, following a simple procedure that should further stimulate local innovation and the growth of an indigenous defence industrial base. The DRDO has also posted a host of military and dual use technologies that the private sector can licence from the DRDO. These are commendable efforts at building the national defence technology and industrial base and it is clear that the DRDO has a highly talented and motivated resource pool of qualified scientists and technicians, well-equipped laboratories and a leadership determined to take our country forward.

The pertinent question we must try to answer now is: What more can India *ask* the DRDO to do to realize the technological aspirations of a New India?

Whilst the nation has a clearly articulated developmental agenda, it is incumbent that our borders remains secure and our forces are equipped with contemporary equipment to deter any belligerency that may derail our developmental goals and targets. Therefore, the first 'ask' is to achieve and retain technological asymmetry over our potential rivals by mastering disruptive technologies.

In warfare, several precedents of technological asymmetry are apparent. Industry 1.0 replaced sails and wooden hulls with steam and steel, and cannons and guns made swordsmen and cavalry redundant. With the advent of the railroad, the wagon industry went bust and steam ships made sail-makers obsolete, whilst guns and cannons replaced spears, sword and shields. Industry 2.0 introduced electric power and revolutionized sensors and communications systems which extinguished the oil-fired lantern and candles business. Industry 3.0 brought in digital technologies that had broad-spectrum applications and was characterized by a fusion of technologies impacting not just a specific sector but multifarious industries.

These technological interventions had a disruptive character that changed the goal post, the conduct of the game itself and challenged the sustaining and incremental model of improvements over established technologies and industrial capability. As the world stands at the threshold of Industry 4.0, it is once again a new basket of disruptive technologies that will impact machinery, weapons, equipment, sensors and communications that our forces must possess to preserve peace and prevail in war.

These disruptive technologies can be clubbed in several ways.

Foremost are technologies that drive military surveillance and communications. Terahertz electronics, nano-technology, smart materials and bio-computational and quantum computing techniques on the one hand, and with miniaturization and MEMS-based sensors on the other, together with combined with machine learning/associated intelligence algorithms and the Internet of Everything (IoE) would radically transform surveillance means and methodologies. For communications, high throughput, secure and encrypted satellite communications, big data analytics, machine learning and robotics, and new methods of securely sharing operational information through enterprise-grade security architectures and techniques of cloud computing are futuristic technological innovations that would also disrupt the existing model of data transfer, information sharing and command, control and communications. In this sector the DRDO could explore developing the highest level of competence in blockchain and artificial intelligence technologies for encrypted communications, surveillance systems and indeed even for manufacturing process control. These technologies also have significant civilian applications and the nation would benefit from these efforts.

The second set of disruptive technologies pertain to advanced materials comprising ultra-powerful, ultra-light, ultra-conductive man-made metals, that can combine to create meta materials, polymers, alloys and composites leading to revolutionary refinements in additive manufacturing using three-dimensional printing (3D Printing). These materials and manufacturing methods will possibly develop asymmetries through more survivable, sustainable and lethal weapon systems. I understand that DRDO is already engaged in the development of new materials such as Carbon Nano Tubes (CNT) and graphene. For the DRDO it would be desirable to detect these signals of alarm impacting not only the present defence industrial base but also determine pointers to a future national industrial base.

Autonomous-vehicles, leveraging new innovations in robotics, automation and miniaturisation and artificial intelligence would open up a third basket of major asymmetry in equipment and, in turn, on conduct of military operations. It is probably the key disruptive technology since it will transfer risk from soldiers employed in hazardous operations to machines, thus fundamentally redefining the art of the possible in future combat operations that are not daunted by the prospect of casualties. Commanders, unburdened from losing their men during operations, can completely re-envision battle plans, logistics and transportation models by exploiting autonomous platforms for ISR and launch of precision-guided weapons. In the future, it is possible to imagine autonomous aircraft, mine hunters, surface craft and underwater vehicles sailing into harm's way at least risk, thus opening never-before options of non-contact warfare creating war-winning asymmetries in asset risk and operational rewards. In this sector the DRDO could explore new technology to provide much longer endurance, greater range of operations and through more and more sophisticated payloads to deliver superior surveillance and combat outcomes by using unmanned vehicles. Potentially the same technology could find applications in road transportation and certainly as we have seen in the railways sector.

A final basket of disruptive technologies is in the field of transformational energy generation and storage systems. We are already seeing advances in battery storage systems which I believe have applications in submarines. We are also seeing rapidly evolving propulsion technology, which may render gas turbines and diesel engines obsolete as they are replaced with fuel cells, wind- and solar-powered turbines, electric propulsion motors, high-capacity and rapid-recharge batteries, hydrogen and fuel cells and even mini nuclear reactors. Here, I would urge that since the country is moving towards electric vehicles and the eventual demise of internal combustion technology is possible, the DRDO work on developing the post-lithium ion generation of solid state batteries, which hold the promise of lighter weight, greater energy storage and faster recharging times. These are, again, dual-use items, and military troop and cargo transport vehicles could be the base on which India's solid state battery research and development could be built, paving the way for the rapid promotion of electric vehicles in India with no lithium or hydrocarbon dependency.

The second 'ask' would be for the DRDO to review its own role in the national development narrative by identifying its 'new' core business. Having walked this long and arduous journey of developing weapons and systems for the armed forces, the time may have come for the DRDO to concentrate more on fundamental research rather than on applied research and system integration. If India has to become a world power in the manufacture of ahead-of-the-art defence products, its research base has to be built on sound knowledge and pushing the frontiers of scientific knowledge first; next, design and engineering skills, which is an integration of scientific knowledge; then come technology solutions that integrate engineering knowledge from several disciplines; and, finally, to develop a product that integrates several technologies.

Across this spectrum, science and engineering are related to fundamental research. Indian industry has matured and applied research and system integration should be more their preserve, freeing the DRDO to concentrate on the advancement of fundamental science and engineering knowledge. Whilst the DRDO could nurture and develop this capability in Indian industry to yet greater heights, I believe that the new frontier that the DRDO must master in the years to come is to develop and own world-class patents and processes, our scientists at DRDO must aspire to be future Nobel laureates in physics and chemistry or even bio sciences in a defined time span and, over time, DRDO-owned patents and licences should make it a profit centre for the central government. This can only be achieved by teaming institutes of technology with DRDO labs to work towards specific outcomes. I must add that these efforts must be agnostic to success and failure being only incidental to the research process itself, which would provide new knowledge.

The third 'ask' would be to reconsider its focus. There is no argument that the DRDO's primary focus must be the defence sector. But having grown to its present stature of a highly talented scientific pool of scientists and state-of-the-art labs and testing facilities, this cannot remain its only focus. A host of disruptive technologies that I mentioned earlier are dual use and the DRDO could consider ways and means that these dual-use, disruptive technologies can generate new industries and ventures that would position India as a lead player in, say, automobiles, electronics, pharma, etc. Some of them I have mentioned earlier. Therefore, the list of products and technologies on offer to the industry to licence and manufacture should be extended to include other potential commercial applications across a variety of industries.

A fourth 'ask' could be to rearticulate the DRDO mission so as to increasingly engage the DRDO resource base to solve a multitude of technological challenges that face the whole of India today and not limited to the aero and defence sector per se. For example, farm stubble burning is a problem that 'crops up' year after year and with no solution in sight. Perhaps the CVRDE and R&D Engineers Pune, for example, can get together with say the Govind Ballabh Pant Agriculture University to jointly design a suitable machine/agricultural implement that would convert the burden of stubbles into benefit for our farmers? Another example could be to develop new materials and methods to replace brick and mortar construction of dwelling units under the Prime Minister Awas Yojana and provide low-cost, high-technology, water-free toilets under Swachh Bharat programme working with the CBRI or an IIT. Unmanned vehicles and payloads for civil and commercial applications are yet another avenue where DRDO expertise can join the national cause. These have applications across agriculture, mining, forests, fisheries, railways, highways and waterways etc. and can transform the ease, cost and way of doing business.

There can be many other PAN-Indian challenges that require Indian solutions and many of them can indeed come from DRDO laboratories and scientists. However, while none of these programmes should impinge on defence projects, there is an obvious need to see how these technologies and missions can be adopted in the civil sector too.

A fifth and final 'ask' would be for greater outreach to Young India. We at NITI Aayog have launched thousands of Atal Tinkering labs in various schools from Mizoram to Maharashtra. NITI Aayog has also commissioned Atal Incubation Centres across the country. These are designed to increase the scientific temperament in Indian society and promote start-ups and entrepreneurs to engage in high-technology business ventures. Startup India, under the DIPP, offers much support to develop the entrepreneurial fabric of New India. We could explore how NITI Aayog, DIPP and DRDO can jointly work together to develop innovation, entrepreneurship and the defence and aerospace industry supply chain through start-ups and the SME route. Both institutions can consider to jointly engage youth at school and college levels, and other entrepreneurs through pitch competitions and ideation enclaves to solve tomorrow's technological challenges today.

In conclusion, I believe it is clear that the path towards a New India at 2022 cannot be walked alone by any entity, however resourceful and gifted that it may be. All of us have to not only put our resources, talents and energy to this national task but also ask ourselves what more can we do together for our country's rapid modernization. We will soon be amongst the top five economies and we need to develop products and processes that would ensure acceptability in global markets, as that is a necessity for employment generation and export-led growth. Perhaps, we should together address the lucrative defence shipbuilding and aircraft market with top-quality products at competitive prices. The challenge would be to develop new technologies and find the right balance of the kind of investments that would need to be made for the future, such that MRO, upgrades and life-extension facilities continue to sustain legacy equipment whilst disruptive technologies are incubated, innovated and introduced for preparing the national industrial base to global standards.

If we have to move out of our comfort zones and respective silos of work and responsibility, then so be it. The DRDO has a tremendous potential to transform India and spearhead the task of nation building.

# Unlimited Potential for the Navy to Reinvent

Legend has it that when Sir Thomas Roe approached Emperor Jehangir for permission to set up a factory at Surat under the Emperor's protection, Empress Noor Jehan, astute as she was, advised the Emperor to decline the request since the Mughal Empire already had great shipbuilding skills, outstanding sailors, fancy merchandise and shrewd traders, and instead urged the Emperor to despatch his fleet to trade and set up establishments in England and Europe. Unfortunately, the suggestion was rejected and that small English factory at Surat became England's first stronghold in India in 1615. Consequently, India missed the industrial revolution of mass manufacture, steel and steam and became an English colony of peasants and artisans.

Most maritime commentators ascribe India's loss of freedom to the sea blindness of the Mughals for whom the predominant threat was from the North. Unfortunately, the soft underbelly of the Indian peninsula with open access through the coasts to India's hinterland, proved India's undoing. Of course, Shivaji and the Zamorins put up valiant fights against the European invaders but inadequate technology and force levels lost India's command over the Arabian sea and, in turn, its very independence.

Post-independence the nation learnt its lessons from history. Whilst the Army and Air Force were downsized, the cabinet accepted, in the early years of independence, that India's future navy should be centred on two carriers with 138 other ships and crafts—a force level that regrettably is yet to be reached even after 70 years.

A ship epitomizes not just the sovereign authority of the state but is a visible manifestation of a nation's industrial might, its technical and managerial skills and its entrepreneurial character. The Indian Navy has been at the forefront of the Make in India initiative since the first Indian-built modern ship, the INS Ajay, was inducted into service in 1961. The Indian Navy is truly a builder's Navy, having inducted close to 130 warships and ordering another 41 ships on Indian shipyards, which is a matter of great satisfaction for all of us. Even today the recent inductions of corvettes, frigates and destroyers are prime examples of the Navy's march towards developing indigenous capability.

In the last several years, a slew of initiatives have been taken to further stimulate Make in India. First, shipping and defence are both identified as strategic sectors for the rapid growth of the national industrial base. In support of this requirement, the Government has promulgated a series of measures to stimulate private sector investment in the sector. To name a few, these include MoD sharing the Technology Perspective and Capability Road map (TPCR) with industry; and the DRDO's Long Term Technology Perspective Plan, which enumerated various requirements for the defence industrial sector. The list of Defence items requiring industrial licence was pruned down to only 16 categories, the process streamlined and validity of licence extended from seven years to 15 years with a provision to further extend it by three years. Since the launch of the Make in India initiative in September 2014, more than 300 licences have been issued for promoting defence sector manufacturing. During the last three financial years, more than 100 procurement proposals worth about `5,50,000 crore have been approved by DAC. In November 2015, FDI up to 49 per cent was allowed through the automatic route and above 49 per cent under Government route on case-to-case basis. JVs that can achieve a minimum of 30 per cent indigenous content for their products, were made exempt from offset obligations. Exchange Rate Variation (ERV) protection was extended to all Indian companies. Anomalies in excise duty/custom duty were removed and all Indian industries (public and private) became subject to the same kind of excise and custom duty levies. Post GST, the regime is equally applicable for both private and public sector.

A defence security manual for defence manufacturing units was promulgated, Outsourcing and Vendor Development Guidelines for SoEs were promulgated to increase outsourcing from private sector including SMEs, and a Technology Development Fund under the DRDO is in place. At NITI Aayog there is potential for investment in innovation through the Atal Innovation Mission. In fact the navy can consider tapping into this fund for promoting tinkering labs in its training facilities.

A defence export strategy was put in place and items that no longer required approval for exports were notified, a Standard Operating Procedure (SOP) for the issue of No Objection Certificate (NOC) and requirement of End User Certificate

(EUC) shared and, a provision for issuing advance/in principle clearance for exploring business opportunities abroad was also allowed. DRDO also issued a compendium of its products having export potential to help Indian industries to explore the potential export market. A National Manufacturing Policy with the objective of enhancing the share of manufacturing in GDP to 25 per cent and creating 100 million jobs over a decade or so has been promulgated, which also seeks state participation. Government is pushing exports through the Line of Credit route for defence goods; and, DIPP has also issued a Public Procurement (Make in India) order in June 2017.

Towards further promoting growth in the sector, NITI Aayog has recommended that nominations for shipbuilding projects (including projects for which RFPs have not been issued) and the requirement of previous experience should be discontinued to entail real price discovery and prevent highly unaffordable time and cost overruns in shipbuilding projects which have been as much as 600 per cent of the cost and thrice the projected acquisition period in some cases. It is time to open the shipbuilding sector to larger participation and get better value for money and more importantly, build alternate capabilities.

NITI Aayog has proposed that a key pillar for the success of *Come, Make in India* is demand aggregation coupled with a life cycle production-cum-maintenance agreement for various common use items such as aircraft and helicopters, aero engines, drones etc. which would make a viable business case for investors. For example, the consolidated demand (MHA and MoD) is in excess of 1.1 million small arms (valued at over ₹70,000 crore) by 2032 whereas piecemeal RFPs/RFIs are being issued for a few thousand small arms of different types. This is, therefore, a fit case for strategic partnering with a competitively chosen foreign OEM company for manufacturing the entire variety of hi-tech small arms in India.

The same is true for helicopters for the Army, Navy or Air Force. The Army has selected the Kamov 226, the HAL-built Advanced Light Helicopter and the Apache, the Navy has issued Request for Information for 111 five-tonne twin-engine Naval Utility Helicopters and another for 125 10-tonne Multi Role Helicopters, the Air Force has chosen the Chinook, Apache and the Mi17 as its mainstay fleet in a piecemeal fashion.

Substantial expenditure is being incurred but it's not contributing to India's defence industrial base or jobs or wealth. These ideally should have been all combined into one National Helicopter Building Program. So, these inter-service requirements must be consolidated and strategic partnerships should be built with down-selected companies rather than for a specific platform or a system. Demand aggregation would create the size and scale for Come, Make in India and thus put the substantial defence budget to more productive national measurable outcomes such as FDI inflows, ToT absorption, jobs, exports etc. Strategic partnerships must not be based on a priori paper evaluations alone, but post facto demonstrated outcomes based on aggregated demands and long-term production plans.

It is also believed that DPSUs must maximize outsourcing to the extent possible to the private sector, particularly MSMEs, who are the bedrock of industrial growth. To encourage them, one of the criterions for their annual ratings should be outsourcing targets which the Navy can support.

Also proposed is that the Ministry of Defence examine feasibility of adopting business process re-engineering in defence acquisitions for achieving time compression by adopting a digitized decision-making system and by eliminating multi-stage and multi-layer approvals, reducing tendering categorization from the present 6 (which essentially defines local content and vendor identity, which can be subsumed in the RFP terms itself) to a standard 3 (Global, Limited, Negotiated), and introducing empowered Contract Negotiation Committees whilst keeping the acquisition audit trail transparent. It has also been recommended that benchmarking in the instance of competitive bids be done away with and field trials of proven in-service equipment be replaced with Test certificates. In several meetings, the necessity for promoting local manufacture and building investor confidence in the sector has been strongly emphasized. It is believed this new approach will facilitate faster induction of much-needed equipment, force modernization and industrial growth.

NITI Aayog has undertaken a study of the impact of the GST regime on defence manufacturing and has suggested rationalization of these taxes.

At NITI Aayog, the three-year action agenda 'proposes linking Central government expenditures to future priorities. It suggests shifting the composition of expenditures by allocating a larger proportion of additional revenues that become available over time to high-priority sectors...which includes defence. In its report, NITI has stated:

Defence Capital Expenditure. The allocation towards capital expenditure in defence will increase from around ₹95,000 crore in 2015-16 to about 1,72,500 crore by 2019-20, thereby increasing its share of total expenditure from 5.3 per cent to 6.2 per cent. This is to allow for greater purchase of equipment for the armed forces, keeping in mind the security considerations for the country.

All these discussions and initiatives were aimed to facilitate timely force modernization, building the national defence industrial base and in turn create jobs/capability in India by encouraging local manufacturing over imports. Despite these slew of measures, sops and encouragement, visible growth is not yet apparent in the sector.

Industry claims that DPSUs continue to be nominated/awarded contracts, benchmarking/trials remains subjective, outsourcing targets are unmet, more than 40 projects are languishing at CNC stage for several months, offset procedures do not encourage manufacturing, acquisition timelines are opaque, GST on defence products require rationalization, not a single 'Make' project has reached RFP stage since its introduction in 2011 and FDI remains moribund at US $5.12 million though several foreign companies have publicly stated their intention to Make in India, not simply Make by India or Make for India.

Yet, something remains amiss, and more importantly, the nation demands more. First, is to get more bang for the buck. The substantial defence budget must be leveraged to not only achieve military capability but actively promote the development of the national industrial base through maximum local sourcing, creating local jobs, driving domestic demand and promoting an export market for our home-grown products. The Navy has a highly responsible role—business development if it wishes to achieve these objectives.

Next, the defence business requires size and scale for sustainability on the one hand and predictability and credibility on the other, to make bankable sustainable investments. Size and scale can only be generated through demand aggregation. Aggregation can occur when specifications are not rigidly defended by each service and some flexibility is built in. A case in point is the plethora of RFI for helicopters, unmanned aerial systems, fighter aircraft, small arms, rockets and missiles, radars and EW systems, all of which are also used by the other services in their order of battle. Consolidating these requirements on a Tri-Service basis would provide the largest fillip to industrial growth. I would urge that requirements of civil and commercial sectors be also included to make a very strong business case for investors and for India's aeronautics industry. The Navy could take the lead on the total requirement of helicopters and design a RFP that would competitively down select a strategic partnership with a company (not for an isolated product as DPP 2016 advocates) that would build not only a variety of helicopters for India but also bring in Tier 1 and Tier 2 companies that would make aero-engines, avionics and rotor blades, for example as a composite deal to make India one of the largest manufacturers of helicopters in the world. The opportunity exists now and we must not fritter it away with salami slicing the total demand into part RFPs.

Another case in point is submarines. Instead of ordering 6 submarines at a time on one shipyard, it makes a good national case to select a modular hull form and order all remaining 18 submarines in one tranche so that a national submarine design and production hub is established in perpetuity and not in fits and bursts where talent and infra languish until fresh orders are announced. Examples are Australia, which has ordered 12 submarines in one tranche; Japan, which is building 22 submarines in a series; the US, which has a 50-year build plan for their Virginia class to deliver 2 submarines a year through a process of continuous evolution; or Russia, China or even South Korea, which have adopted an evolving but continuous submarine build programme. I strongly urge that the Navy actively considers closely integrating its submarine acquisition plans with the national industrial base that would create long-term assets, expertise and a comprehensive ecosystem to make India amongst the top submarine builders in the world over a 30- to 40-year continuous submarine-building plan. Piecemeal programmes won't help.

Similarly, drones that have civil and commercial applications could also be led by another service. I recommend that all future programmes be modelled as a long-term production-cum-maintenance concession that provides a long-term visibility for users and investors alike.

Predictability and credibility are offshoots of the adherence to promulgated procedures, timelines and ethics. Predictability is about consistency in procedures and policies that are not changed during an acquisition process such as the promulgated timelines from initiation to contract closure. Retracting RFPs does not instil credibility in the system and is a definitive reflection of inadequate staff work during proposal formulation.

Third, we realize that none of these initiatives can deliver on ground unless the customer—in this case the Indian Navy—becomes a concerned stakeholder in nation-building. Whilst the Services can remain focussed only on their requirements for national security and be agnostic to its source, it behoves one and all to first explore Indian avenues and options of procurement before proceeding to foreign shores. I urge the Navy to be a concerned stakeholder in building India's defence industrial base—not limited to ships and aircraft but also down to systems, equipment and machinery.

Fourth, whilst there can be no dispute that the ultimate outcome is attained when everything is Indian designed, developed and manufactured, the reality is that this is not how the modern global production supply chain works. The offset policy as it stands today discourages long-term manufacture and only promotes limited trading. Specifying local content should be pragmatic and realizable and not be too ambitious. Market forces will drive local content.

Fifth, on the maritime front, the potential of the Blue Economy still remains unrealized. Central Government has initiated several ultra, mega projects such as the Sagarmala, SAGAR, MAUSAM, Coastal Employment Zones, and Island Development Scheme to build 10 world class island resorts, inland waterways etc. where the Navy can potentially provide useful inputs. I truly believe that the potential of the Andaman and Nicobar Islands to become one of the world's busiest transhipment and bunkering hubs, an electronics manufacturing mega centre, a biotech base, a world-class tourist destination etc. is just waiting to be realized. Why can't the Islands become India's Hong Kong and generate at least 0.5 per cent (a ten-fold increase) of India's GDP by 2022? We can set similar aspirational targets for the Lakshadweep Islands. These programmes are run by inter-ministerial groups and various state governments/departments and agencies are stakeholders but the Navy is a key pillar. In fact, we intend to work on a comprehensive Integrated Maritime Policy and Coastal Transformation (IMPACT) Paper where we would be delighted to work with the Navy and its think tanks. I urge that the Navy, as part of its outreach efforts, proactively contributes to the success of these programmes or even innovate new programmes for nation-building.

Then, the Navy is a powerful storehouse of cutting edge and disruptive technologies. The rapid advances in disruptive technologies, specifically in the sector of materials and nanotechnology, robotics, automation and miniaturization, additive manufacturing, big data and computation, energy storage systems etc., are an outcome of defence manufacturing. Potentially, many of these technologies are dual use. I urge that the Navy continue to proactively engage with industry, academia and think tanks—I notice it has had three rounds of 'Make in India' conferences in the last two years, one of which I attended—to guide the growth of the national industrial capability and skill development.

Finally, a traditional peacetime function of navies has been to secure the sea lines of communications and preserve regional stability that would ensure the nations' access to resources, commodities and markets for sustainable national growth and development. For fuels, hydrocarbons are a key current resource and lithium is the future. India's demand for hydrocarbons is likely to grow at a CAGR of 4 per cent for oil and 5 per cent for gas, and despite an investment of $75 billion in upstream, mid-stream and downstream projects India's dependence on imports would be close to 68 per cent—most of which would be transported by ships by 2030. India, today, has no lithium resources and these would need to be imported from South America. The Navy's role would become further important, given the pressures on commodities transit, freedom of navigation in the global oceanic commons, larger incidents of piracy and sea-borne terrorism, pollution, the continuous and increasing presence of China in the Indian Ocean Region and above all, the natural responsibilities that are accruing to India as a net security provider etc. This would require the Navy to redesign its force structure and composition, acquire long-range, all-weather, rapid and combined surveillance and response platforms such as amphibious aircraft, high-end data analytics driven by artificial intelligence and machine language, cyber-proofed networks and a new set of skills.

TWO

# BUSINESS AND ECONOMY

# A Jump in Ease of Doing Business: Fruits of Persistent Efforts

Every year, the *Doing Business* report of World Bank Group ranks economies on the basis of their performance on ten indicators spread across the business lifecycle of a small- and medium-size enterprise. In 2014, our Prime Minister shared his vision of taking India amongst the top 50 countries of the World Bank's *Doing Business* report. At the time, India was ranked 142 out of 189 economies, last among the BRICS nations and sixth among the eight South Asian economies. His objective was to make India easy and simple and enhance the citizens' ease of living.

Today, India's stands at 77 in *Doing Business* 2019, released by the World Bank Group, making us the highest-ranked South Asian nation. In three years, we have improved our ranking by 65 positions—a claim that few countries of India's size and complexity can claim.

But why does improvement on index matter for 'Make in India'? The perception of a country drives business, and the reforms that are implemented demonstrate that we are open for business. The World Bank report highlights the top reformers and rank, based on feedback collected from private sector respondents familiar with them.

Today, India is among the top 25 on three indicators (getting electricity, protecting minority investors and getting credit), and in the top 80 on another two indicators (dealing with construction permits and trading across borders). This remarkable achievement didn't happen overnight, or even in a few months. The improvement reflects continuous efforts of implementing agencies over the last four years to ease the regulatory environment.

This remarkable transformation has been the result of sustained efforts by a number of implementing departments, spanning central, state and municipal governments, to improve on their respective indicators.

The Department of Industrial Policy and Promotion (DIPP) deserves special praise for having pursued this initiative with vigour and energy. These changes in mindset and approach to reform have been critical to achieving the successes that we are celebrating today. These learnings will be especially critical as we strive to focus on further improving our performance on *Doing Business*, with the objective of achieving the Prime Minister's vision of making India the easiest and simplest place to do business in.

Further improvement depends on our ability to drive similar reforms in the indicators where we still lag. Reforms in both enforcing contracts and registering property are the most complex among all the *Doing Business* indicators in the context of India, due to the multiplicity of stakeholders involved. There have been some significant efforts in these areas already—the central government has amended the commercial courts, commercial divisions, and Commercial Appellate Divisions Act, 2015, to allow district court-level commercial courts.

Similarly, the state governments of Delhi and Maharashtra have invested heavily in digitizing land records and building online solutions for registration and mutation.

But these efforts are merely the first steps in the right direction. What these indicators have in common is the time that they take. *Doing Business* indicates it takes more than four years to resolve a commercial dispute, and it takes several weeks to conduct title search on property and to mutate the property into the name of the new owner. The time taken to complete these formalities underlies primarily why we continue to lag when it comes to these indicators.

Technology can play a critical and significant role in reducing the time requirement—digitizing land records can help improve public access, and introducing e-court management systems can smoothen processes through automation.

Similarly, digitizing land records are useful, but they are not effective in isolation. A land buyer checks deeds, land records, cadastral maps, court records, property tax records and mortgages to make sure the land they buy is free of encumbrances. All this information is held in different agencies, at differing stages of digitizing. Instead, we must integrate all this data into a useable, searchable format that allows users to quickly and effectively identify encumbrances through a single interface.

The *Doing Business* report shows that much of the world is reforming, and so, we must also strive to incrementally improve on all the indicators where we do well so that we can continue to maintain our current ranking on these indicators.

What we have learned over the past three years is that, in India, transformative change is possible if we put our minds to it. When we began these efforts, few architects believed that there would be reforms and India would improve its position in the World Bank Index. We have not merely jumped up by 65 positions but created an immense competitive spirit amongst our states by ranking them. We need exactly this spirit to continue with even greater momentum to implement the reforms we need in order to achieve the Prime Minister's vision of earning a rank among the top nations on *Doing Business*. So, while today we celebrate our achievements, from tomorrow we must embark dedicatedly to reform, perform and transform the way we deal with business disputes and land management in India.

# Making India Easy and Simple by Institutionalizing Arbitration

There have been two major initiatives by the Government of India in the last week that will help change the perception of India as a barrier-free destination for conducting business, and proactivity in helping pivot away from the overwhelming pendency in Indian courts. Last week, a bill was passed by the Lok Sabha that facilitates the instituting of the New Delhi International Arbitration Centre (the NDIAC), meant to boost efficacious conduct and management of Alternative Dispute Resolution (ADR) proceedings in India. As an autonomous institution and one that is proposed to be an institute of national importance, the NDIAC will aim at making India the hub for arbitration matters. This, along with the presenting of the Arbitration and Conciliation (Amendment) Bill 2019 before the Rajya Sabha, seeks to make India a hub of domestic and global arbitration for settling commercial disputes. This bill provides for the establishing of the Arbitration Council of India, an independent body empowered to frame rules on grading institutions and setting out norms on accreditation of arbitrators, quality and performance monitoring, and building capacity for arbitrators.

Arbitration is a vitally important supplement to enable and enhance the ease of doing business in India, and in fact, the entire world. It can greatly alleviate the pressure on courts, therefore, reducing pendency, as well as instill investor confidence in India as a hub, if the dispute resolution processes are efficient, expedited and effective. Systematic understanding and usage of arbitration for dispute resolution will solve many existing issues in the current legal framework in India, including reducing the burden on Indian courts, and giving due priority to the economic impact of the outcome of a dispute resolution order.

Pendency in the courts today is a massive concern. The National Judicial Data Grid estimates that there are more than three crore cases pending across courts with approximately 65 lakh cases pending for over five years. The enforcement of contracts as well as the time taken to resolve matters is likely to worry potential investors who otherwise would flock towards investment opportunities in India.

It is, therefore, vital to implementing institutional arbitration in India across sectors and lineage. Until now, arbitrations in India have unfortunately not been conducted in a structured matter. Ad hoc arbitrations usually devolve into the format of a court hearing with the result that adjournments are granted regularly and lawyers too prefer to appear in court rather than completing the arbitration proceeding. One must also strongly reiterate the rebuilding of a robust structured arbitral ecosystem in the country which focuses on institutional arbitration.

Presently, in India, a number of arbitral domestic and international institutions exist; however, there is no single arbitral seat or institution in the country which is a centre of global repute. This is now envisioned with the NDIAC.

Establishing a stable and vibrant ecosystem for the arbitral institution is a significant consideration. The institutions in themselves should be credible, independent, efficient and transparent—a challenge in India, considering its diversity. Further, the leadership of the institution should be vibrant and should be supported by well-trained support staff for qualitative arbitration and library apart from physical and technological infrastructure. Effective use of technology such as e-filing, creating database of cases, big data analytics, online dispute resolution, and video conferencing needs to be scaled up and be put to extensive use in the process of arbitration. By laying out the methodology and processes for appointing and accrediting arbitrators, the legislations should solve the existing issues of capacity and capability. What is needed today is the training of arbitrators, especially for the ones which do not have any judicial background so that the awards passed by them can withstand judicial scrutiny. This would help in not only generating specialized professionals but would also ensure that arbitration does not take a back seat as compared to litigation in court.

Messaging is critical. Promoting arbitration, and thus, preventing the tendency of private players to rush to the courts without resorting to the relevant provisions of arbitration in the contract, whereby the commencement/continuation of the work was stalled, is a concern. This can be handled by creating awareness for better understanding of commercial matters and an ecosystem wherein the awards are passed by neutral umpires to ensure that it is a win-win situation for all the stakeholders. This would leave a limited scope of the award being challenged under Section 34 of the Arbitration Act, 1996.

India is diligently working on establishing confidence in its legal system which is the fundamental condition for any country to become an international arbitration venue. Over the past four years, a number of legislative and executive changes have been brought about, in addition to the most recent developments. The amendments to the Arbitration and Conciliation Act were passed in 2015 to make the arbitration process user-friendly, cost-effective, and to ensure speedy disposal. Indian arbitral institutions must now demonstrate that they are integrated with international arbitration institutions so that they can deliver effective arbitration work at a lower cost. All major Indian cities are already equipped with the requisite technological infrastructure and linguistic capability. We also have extremely able practitioners with holistic multi-jurisdictional experience and competencies.

India will not have a robust domestic arbitration environment unless institutional arbitration becomes mandatory. This can only be done if arbitration agreements mention the specific institution that will conduct arbitral proceedings. Once domestic arbitration becomes popular through institutional arbitration, it will eventually lead to international commercial arbitrations being conducted in India. To promote India as a business and arbitral destination, the government contracts ought to have a neutral arbitration institution in all their contracts. All public sector undertakings may mandatorily have a clause for institutional arbitration that should provide arbitration through an arbitration institution. In order to promote India as an arbitrational hub, this arbitral institution should be indigenous.

Institutional arbitration will ensure loosening of the stranglehold that pendency has on enforcement of contracts and other legal delays. The Government of India has made major strides in greater efficiency and efficacy in resolving commercial disputes, including major legislative measures on promoting ADR. With top-class arbitration as an alternative, many of the concerns regarding enforcement and delays in the courts will likely dissipate. Until businesses, both Indian and global, have access to timely dispute resolution and are not afraid of unlimited pendency and delays, India's full potential as a progressive economy will remain unfulfilled. Maximum justice and minimum delay is the vision that the Government of India has. Institutionalized arbitration will go a long way towards ensuring this, as part of a New India by 2022.

# The Inspirational Story of an Aspirational District: Dantewada

Dantewada in Chhattisgarh is one of the 115 districts covered by the recently launched Aspirational Districts Programme. Covering an area of 3450 sq. km with a population of 2.83 lakh residents, as per the 2011 census, Dantewada is in the Left Wing Extremism (LWE) region that has seen significant adversity, including violence and living under the constant threat of extremists on a daily basis. The geographical layout of Dantewada is such that the terrain is covered by forests (over 60 per cent) and otherwise difficult to access. The agriculture is somewhat less developed due to various factors, and there has traditionally been dependence on gathering from the forests. But Dantewada is overcoming massive obstacles and moving towards a complete transformation. For, what Dantewada has in abundance is an unsurpassable sense of spirit and purpose, and coupled with a generous dose of innovative ability, Dantewada's is a story of inspiration, where spirit trumps adversity.

I have recently visited Dantewada and seen first-hand the incredible strides that have been made in literacy, health, gainful employment, incentivizing initiative, and even a public-private partnership in the form of a BPO operating on profit-making fundamentals and using comparative advantages. This ingenuity is through a positive mindset despite the odds and ground reality, along with a stubborn refusal to be intimidated by the LWE that surrounds them.

The district has an Education City that houses 18 institutions, a project that KPMG has ranked as among the 100 best innovative infrastructures in the world. Despite the anti-development stance of the LWE, the Education City continues to educate and find new ways for innovative processes. With a total capacity for 5,500 students, Education City offers a gamut of options. Aastha Vidya Mandir provides residential CBSE schooling from Classes I to XII in an English-medium curriculum, free of charge. One-third of the students are children who have been impacted by LWE violence. It also houses a school for children with special needs, a sports facility, a polytechnic institute, and a vocational/livelihood college. 'Choo Lo Aasmaan' is another landmark initiative, bringing in students of Classes XI and XII to receive coaching for medical and engineering college entrance exams.

The Education City also houses a PPP-driven BPO called 'Yuva', managed by Hyderabad-based Sixth Generation Technologies. With the goal of providing 1,000 youngsters jobs at a salary of ₹8,000-14,000, with Indian and MNC clients, this is a truly remarkable achievement. It is a precedent for every other aspirational district in the country.

In an initiative that was recently launched, Dantewada has announced a scheme of women's ownership and driving e-rickshaws. These e-rickshaws cost approximately ₹1.60 lakh with 20 per cent of the funding for each rickshaw to be borne by the self-help groups, and the remaining 80 per cent is borne by the District Mineral Foundation (DMF). DMF is an initiative set up in all districts impacted by mining operations. The DMF aims to work for the interest and benefit of persons in these areas, and is funded through the contributions from miners by allocating a certain percentage from the royalty payments. In this case, DMF is benefitting the e-rickshaw initiative, the purpose of which is to enhance, and in many cases, create connectivity from nearby villages that are providing access, a safer mode of transportation, and building an income stream for the rickshaw drivers who must only be women. There are already nearly 150 such e-rickshaws operating. The number of women who have been trained to drive are nearly 1,500, so this initiative is scalable.

A similar contributory assistance programme involves a district-level initiative, with women of the district being given the option to raise Kadaknath chickens—a breed found in this region that is distinctive in its colour (black) and its high-protein meat. Raising these chickens and selling them is also a lucrative activity as they command significantly higher prices than regular chicken. Under this initiative, women are being given Kadaknath chicks at a heavily reduced cost, with the money they earn from the business to be used to enhance their family's quality of life whether through rain-proofing homes, sending their family members to college or just simply having some extra income for basic necessities. Other such initiatives that provide welcome income to women here are operating mini rice-mills from home, and growing mushrooms.

There's more. A completely homegrown effort by the authorities has been made to create a free-WiFi zone around a small area where shops are located to make it a cashless digital zone through micro-innovation. Also noteworthy is

'Bhoomgadi', an organic farmer's producer company owned by 1,600 farmers, marketing their products under the brand name 'Aadim'.

The huge strides taken have been enabled by some of the young and determined district collectors over the past few years. Om Prakash Choudhary, K.C. Devasenapathi and present district collector, Saurabh Kumar, have led from the front. Extremely laudable is the role played by the state government which has delegated the responsibility and authority in a significant way to the young collectors, and the results are there for all to see.

I frequently stress on the need for ease of doing business and for creating an environment that fosters entrepreneurship and innovation. In Dantewada, despite conditions that have been far from conducive to the entrepreneurial spirit, the individuals and institutions are not only acting with zeal and vigour but also embarking on ventures that enhance comparative advantage and provide goods and services that have significant value addition. It just goes to show that the spirit and drive cannot be suppressed no matter how difficult external factors may be. That the entrepreneurial ventures are driven by women, at times even literally as in the case of e-rickshaws, makes this as inspirational as any other factor of success.

I am confident that through groundbreaking benefits that will result from the transformation of Aspirational Districts Programme, the efforts of the state government of Chhattisgarh to push in reform, and projects by Government of India such as the Pradhan Mantri Gram Sadak Yojana (PMGSY), which will improve linkage to all 35 districts affected by LWE to the national highway network, are measures that will greatly enhance the quality of life of the people of districts like Dantewada. The Dantewada experience is a precursor for the Aspirational Districts initiative that synergizes, harmonizes and optimizes. This may only be the beginning of a long journey, but what a beginning it is. A truly inspirational story from one of our aspirational districts.

# The Imperative of Make in India

'Make in India' has completed its anniversary last month and the overall economic environment for India appears far more positive and opportunistic than for the world as a whole. Forecasts from The International Monetary Fund (IMF), World Bank and Japanese brokerage firm Nomura indicate that India is growing at around 7.5–8 per cent this fiscal year, with possibilities for positive revisions as the reforms gradually show results. E&Y's survey of 2015 has ranked India as the most attractive market. It also states that India has emerged as the number one foreign direct investment (FDI) destination in the world during the first half of 2015. This survey reconfirms the earlier findings of *Financial Times*, London, which had also placed India ahead of China for Greenfield FDIs in 2015. Frost & Sullivan, in its global study of growth, innovation and leadership has placed India at number one position amongst hundred countries. Similarly, *Foreign Policy Magazine* of the USA has ranked India at number one position in the list of the world's topmost destinations amongst 110 countries. India today is an oasis of growth in the midst of a barren economic landscape.

The recent GDP numbers show that India registered a growth of 7 per cent in the first quarter of 2015–16, lower than 7.5 during the same period last year. The overall GDP number, which is a cause of worry for some, is the fastest in the world. This is impressive amidst the IMF concerns of lower global growth in the first half of 2015 owing to further slowdown in emerging economies and a weaker recovery in advanced economies, as highlighted in the recent report for G20 Meeting on 'Global Prospects and Policy Challenges'.

The latest data on Index of Industrial Production (IIP) for the month of August shows a healthy growth of 6.4 per cent, after growing at more than 4 per cent in June and July. Manufacturing, in particular, grew at around 6.9 per cent in August. The cumulative growth of IIP from April to August 2015 is around 4.1 per cent, higher than 3 per cent during the corresponding period last year. Other macroeconomic indicators, such as inflation, fiscal deficit, current account deficit and foreign exchange reserves have also shown significant improvement in the last one year.

Despite the recent global turbulences, both the short-term and long-term growth prospects remain favourable.

## CREATING A ROBUST MANUFACTURING SECTOR: 'MAKE IN INDIA' INITIATIVE

In India, the manufacturing sector is small as compared to that of other BRICS (Brazil, Russia, India, China and South Africa) nations. It accounts for just 17.2 per cent of GVA at current basic prices. Raising the share of manufacturing in GDP in India has become the priority because of the enormous potential that the manufacturing sector has for generating higher inclusive growth with enormous opportunities to the workforce. Without manufacturing growing at a faster rate, job absorption would continue to be low.

Countries worldwide are increasingly organizing their production, trade and investment decisions based on opportunities provided by the global value chains, and are signing bilateral and multilateral trade agreements with one another, to more often than not, avoid any disadvantage from exclusion. Success, today, depends principally on how countries are able to compete on cost, quality and productivity in the manufacturing sector.

With this backdrop, the 'Make in India' programme was introduced with the objective to bring the manufacturing sector at the centre stage of economic growth in India and to develop India as a hub for manufacturing design and innovation. Twenty-five sectors have been identified as thrust sectors of the 'Make in India' programme.

Action-plans for 25 thrust sectors has been finalized and a professional agency is currently engaging with nodal officers of these ministries/departments on a regular basis to assist them in setting time frames to monitor targets listed out in the action plan and submit progress report.

## BUILDING A CONDUCIVE AND ENABLING ENVIRONMENT

Various ease-of-doing-business initiatives have been undertaken to de-licence and deregulate the industry during the entire life cycle of a business. (Details of initiatives taken on ease of doing business are given in the Annexure.) DIPP is also closely working with the state governments in helping them identify constraints in doing business and improving the overall business environment in their respective states. A 98-point questionnaire for ascertaining the status of existing policy and procedures impacting the setting up of industries/ business as per an action plan was shared by DIPP with the states. Based on the responses received, an assessment framework for ranking states on the basis of implementation of business reforms was completed and results have been released by World Bank last month to provide a roadmap to states and help them learn from one another and replicate success stories.

An expert committee is examining the possibility of replacing multiple prior permissions with pre-existing regulatory mechanism. Public comments on various suggestions received by them are being invited.

On the recommendation of the Law Commission of India, a Commercial Courts Bill 2015, which provides for setting up of commercial divisions in high courts which exercise original jurisdiction, and commercial courts for dealing with commercial disputes, has been introduced in the Parliament. This is expected to improve India's performance in enforcing contracts relating to cases such as intellectual property rights, arbitration, insurance and taxation.

These measures will increase profitability of firms and hence encourage investor confidence and further investments.

## FOCUS ON INFRASTRUCTURE:

The success of 'Make in India' is intrinsically linked with the overall infrastructure environment of the economy which is our prime focus.

Our stress is on building a pentagon of industrial corridors to boost manufacturing (Delhi-Mumbai industrial corridor, Chennai-Bengaluru industrial corridor, Bengaluru-Mumbai industrial corridor, Amritsar-Kolkata industrial corridor and Vizag-Chennai industrial corridor). A lot of care is taken to engage stakeholders at every stage in discussions, state government's views and priorities are fully accounted for and industries most suitable along different corridors are being identified. The work related to planning, coordination, funding, development, etc. of these industrial corridors is to be handled by the National Industrial Corridor Development Authority which is being created.

The creation of National Investment and Infrastructure Fund (NIIF) is also underway, the framework for which was recently released. The fund will be crucial in infusing equity capital in the infrastructure finance companies, which can further be leveraged manyfold. Once operational, fresh investments in green-field and brown-field projects and support to existing cash-starved stalled projects would be ensured.

## LIBERAL AND INVESTOR-FRIENDLY INVESTMENT POLICY

Under the programme, an investor facilitation cell has been created in 'Invest India' to guide, assist and hand-hold investors during the entire life cycle of the business. Some states have also created an investor facilitation cell. Country-specific help desks are being created to cater to the need of specific investors.

The government has put in place an investor-friendly policy on FDI which is reviewed on an ongoing basis to make it more investor-friendly. Various measures have been taken to liberalize the FDI policy—caps on FDI have been raised in the defence sector, insurance sector and pension sector from 26 per cent to 49 per cent, FDI has been permitted in operation and maintenance in specified rail infrastructure projects, and norms have been revised for 100 per cent FDI under automatic route in construction along with exempting medical devices from sectoral restrictions for pharmaceuticals. Further, composite caps on all forms of foreign investments have also been introduced recently to provide uniformity and simplicity across the sectors in FDI policy for attracting foreign investments. We are going a step forward now by launching the next generation of FDI reforms where the focus is at cutting the need for prior government approval and simplification of the overall FDI policy so as to reduce any delays in approvals.

The continuous efforts to reinstall investors' confidence have started gradually translating into outcomes. FDI equity inflow into the economy has increased by about 27 per cent during 2014–15, and about 31 per cent during April and June 2015, corresponding to the same period last year.

According to UNCTAD's World Investment Report 2015, India regained its position in the list of top 10 destinations for FDI in 2014. India's rank as a top prospective host country for FDI rose to third place from fourth place.

As per a recently announced World Economic Forum's Global Competitiveness Report 2015–16, India's rank improved 16 positions, to 55th position from 71st in that time period. The ranking is based on the performance on 114 indicators that are clubbed in 12 parameters such as infrastructure, macroeconomic environment, institutions, market size and innovation, among others. India ranks well in market size, institutions, business sophistication, innovation, etc. and almost all parameters have shown improvement in the last one year.

## PROMOTING SKILL DEVELOPMENT

India is one of the youngest nations in the world with more than two-thirds of the total population below 35 years of age and we are quite suitable for becoming a manufacturing hub. We have young people, but these youths are unemployable as they lack the required skill sets for meaningful economic employment. Today, less than 5 per cent of India's potential workforce gets formal skill training to be employable and stay employable.

The presence of a skilled workforce is the backbone of the manufacturing sector and overall development of the economy. The government has taken a number of steps to enhance the skills, thereby improving the employability of workers/unemployed in India.

To make India a skill capital of the world, the 'Skill India' initiative has recently been launched. Under this, various initiatives have been introduced, such as providing an umbrella framework to all skilling activities under the National Policy for Skill Development and Entrepreneurship 2015, a flagship scheme of Pradhan Mantri Kaushal Vikas Yojana (PMKVY), with financial rewards to complete skill training, recognition of training and prior learning skills by issuing recognizable certificates and financial assistance to youths seeking to attend skill development programmes under Skill Loan Scheme.

Existing and potential companies can immensely benefit from the presence of skilled workforce.

## PROMOTING AND NURTURING INNOVATION AND ENTREPRENEURSHIP

India is also creating an encouraging ecosystem to support entrepreneurship and start-ups.

A techno-financial, incubation and facilitation programme, called SETU (Self-Employment and Talent Utilisation), has been announced by the Prime Minister to support all aspects of start-up businesses and other self-employment activities, particularly in technology-driven areas.

In order to create an ecosystem conducive for venture capital in the Micro, Small and Medium Enterprises (MSME) sector, a fund for funds, called 'India Aspiration Fund', has been set up under Small Industries Development Bank of India (SIDBI). The fund will attract private capital by way of providing equity, soft loans, other risk capital, etc. to various venture funds which will then come up with newer investment ideas and protocols.

With a special focus on 25 thrust sectors of 'Make in India', SIDBI 'Make in India' Loan for Small Enterprises (SMILE) has been launched to offer quasi-equity and term-based short-term loans to Indian SMEs with less stringent rules and regulations.

To further support the financing and development needs of micro-units and existing small businesses, a Micro Units Development Refinance Agency (MUDRA) bank has been set up which will provide development and refinance to commercial banks/non-banking financial companies/cooperative banks for loans given to micro-units. The bank will follow a credit-plus approach in the form of providing financial literacy, addressing skill gaps, information gaps, etc.

India has a pool of young, talented, enthusiastic creative innovators. A strong intellectual property regime promotes creativity and develops the culture of respect for innovations and creativity in the country. Several measures have been taken to ensure continuous and unending improvement of the Indian intellectual property (IP) ecosystem. IP offices have been radically transformed and human resources have been augmented. Incentivized online filing facilities have been provided with concessions for MSMEs to encourage Indian entrepreneurs to innovate.

AIM has been launched as an innovation promotion platform, involving academics, entrepreneurs and researchers, drawing upon national and international experiences to foster a culture of innovation and R&D in India. The platform will also promote a network of world-class innovation hubs. The mission will provide funds to a network of institutions to conduct research on innovations and will be a mechanism to promote an exchange of ideas.

## CONNECTING DIGITALLY

Digital India aims to reform government systems, eliminate waste, increase access and empower citizens. It will drive the next wave of growth, which will be knowledge-driven. Broadband in every village, with a wide range of online services, will transform India in a manner we cannot foresee.

Besides digital connectivity, measures such as proposed GST (economic connectivity), providing thrust to infrastructure in general, and developing new smart cities and industrial clusters in identified industrial corridors (physical connectivity) are working towards making India a barrier-free well-connected national market for seamless movement of goods and services across state. The Sagarmala Project is one such initiative.

## CHALLENGES

There are several challenges of factor market reforms. India's labour laws are antiquated; its land laws impact infrastructure development severally. Despite several measures, there is a need for greater consistency, predictability and clarity in our tax policies. There is also a need to improve our regulatory mechanisms.

## CONCLUSION

The reforms that have been initiated in the past one year or so have created an optimistic and positive environment for business, investors and budding entrepreneurs. As a result, a number of domestic and international companies are setting up or seriously planning to set up manufacturing facilities in India. A ground for business-friendly and sustained growth is set. The direction is right. We just need to accelerate this growth.

# Export or Perish: Why India Must Increase Exports to Drive Growth

A quantum jump in exports presents a tremendous opportunity for India. Nearly two-thirds of the world's production takes place in global value chains (GVCs). Integrating with these supply chains will not only bring welfare gains, but they will also help increase efficiency and drive growth. The conditions are ripe for India to enhance exports to boost economic growth.

India's economy cannot grow on a sustained basis without exports. In 2017–18, exports of goods and services contributed about 12 per cent of India's GDP. In contrast, exports made up over 42 per cent of South Korea's GDP. Similarly, in 2006, when China was growing at nearly 13 per cent, the share of exports in GDP was more than 37 per cent. For India to achieve double-digit growth, exports will be a crucial part of the strategy.

Although India's exports have been rising of late, there remains ample room for further growth. In 2017–18, exports of goods and services grew by nearly 13 per cent. The last month witnessed the highest month-on-month increase in exports in the last six months. Exports grew by over 20 per cent in May

2018 compared to May 2017. It seems as if the dip in exports witnessed over the last five years may be behind us. This is an opportune time to shift gears and pursue exports more aggressively, building on the government's existing initiatives.

## DON'T LET THE URGENT OVERSHADOW THE IMPORTANT: FOCUS ON SCALE

Several measures, such as ensuring exporters receive GST refunds for raw materials in a timely manner, are undoubtedly critical to raising exports in the short term. At the same time, though, higher exports must be sustained in the medium and long term. This will not be possible if we don't remove the barriers to firms' scaling up. Larger firms not only witness lower per-unit costs, but they also benefit from global competition that drives them to increase the productivity levels continuously. We don't need to look far from home to see this in practice. India's automotive sector has been successful in large part due to the ability of domestic firms to scale up.

Promoting clusters and zones of production will facilitate firms becoming larger. The government is focusing on manufacturing clusters, especially around coastal areas so that exports can be dispatched faster given their proximity to ports. Cluster-based manufacturing will allow firms to save on costs while the location close to coastal areas will save transportation cost and time. In 2010–11, 72 per cent of India's manufacturing workforce was employed in firms with less than 20 workers each. However, they contributed less than 12 per cent in the manufacturing output. Removing barriers faced by MSME with respect to accessing capital, hiring workers and acquiring land will help these firms expand and increase productivity.

## EASE OF DOING BUSINESS

In 2017, India ranked 146 out of 190 economies in the World Bank's 'trading across borders' component of doing business, which measures the time and cost (excluding tariffs) associated with documentary and border compliance and domestic transport procedures for trading goods. Indian exporters on average took nearly four times the time taken by Chinese exporters to comply with border compliance requirements in 2017.

We can reduce border and port turnaround times and lower the cost of trading through a number of measures. First, we need to focus on digitization across ports. Last-mile online access and moving processes completely online will help cut down compliance times drastically. Second, we should ensure that major non-Electronic Data Interchange (EDI) ports are converted to EDI ports urgently for faster clearances. The EDI message exchange system facilitates documentation-related activities such as authorizations across departments. Third, we must ensure policy consistency to reduce informational barriers and facilitate exports. The Central Board of Excise and Customs (CBEC) issued approximately 173 tariff-related notifications between 1 April 2015 and 27 June 2018. The large number of additional notifications increases the complexity of the trade rules. They also impose additional costs of doing business for domestic and international firms.

States govern many issues related to the ease of doing business. For example, they grant firms electricity and water connections. They also govern property registration. Thus, states play an important role in helping firms operate smoothly and in exporting. Studies have found that Indian states that engage in foreign and inter-state trade tend to be richer than non-exporting states. Thus, states also need to play a major role in boosting exports by easing the business environment, enhancing digitization and strengthening infrastructure and connectivity within their states.

## SETTING STANDARDS

There has been a growing recognition of standards as a driver of trade and technical development. The Ministry of Commerce and Industry has been promoting the use of international standards by Indian exporters, recently releasing the Indian National Strategy for Standardization. Adjusting to these standards will help firms tap into international markets. In certain sectors—such as agriculture and food processing—the lack of compliance with standards has prevented exporters from penetrating markets such as the U.S., E.U. and Japan. Conformity with sanitary and phytosanitary measures will help Indian food products become globally acceptable.

Global standards are continually evolving. In addition to compliance by Indian manufacturing firms, the identification of specific standards and regulations across different sectors by industry bodies and relevant ministries will help India participate in GVCs. Indian firms should ensure that they stay abreast of international developments in the space of standards and technical regulations. Conforming to changes in a timely manner plays a prime role in shaping the market access of Indian goods and services.

Globally, trade tensions are running high. Rising protectionism threatens long-standing economic relations between countries. Existing trade agreements look precarious and ongoing deals are stalled. Yet, there has never been a more important time for India to focus on exports.

# From Cash to Digital Payments: A Transformative Opportunity

Victor Hugo once said, 'No power on Earth can stop an idea whose time has come.' The move of delegalizing currency notes of ₹500 and ₹1000 denomination presents an opportunity for digital payments to radically pick up pace in India. There are several reasons why the uptick of digital payments has historically been slow in India. The value of notes and coins in circulation as a percentage of GDP is 12 per cent in India compared to 3.9 per cent in Brazil, 5.3 per cent in Mexico and 3.7 per cent in South Africa. Mobile payment systems in countries like Kenya (M-Pesa) are used by over two-thirds of their adult population; India still lacks such near-ubiquitous options. This brings us to the question—given the diversity of India's population, what are the various payment modes that can be employed?

There are five low-cost, convenient payment options that people can use. For people with smartphones (approximately 250 million in number) with an ability to self-transact, Unified Payments Interface (UPI), e-Wallets and cards (credit, debit) are digital modes. For people with feature phones (approximately 350 million) who can self-transact, *99# banking (or USSD

Payment) and cards (debit, credit or even prepaid) are digital modes. And for people without a phone or those not yet ready for self-service (approximately 350 million), Aadhaar-enabled payment services (via micro ATMs) and prepaid cards are digital options. Digital payment is an area already rife with technology innovations—'contactless' payment options using sound waves to enable offline, proximity-based payments on any device are unique innovations and easier micro-sized Japanese QR code solutions can also be used for person-to-person payments.

The Government of India has moved to facilitate adoption of these digital payments on mission mode. One of the key areas is increasing awareness of digital payment options in campaign mode working with different stakeholders like RBI, banks, telecom companies, and other fintech companies to de-bottleneck and make current payment modes simpler to operate. UPI is being made interoperable, and USSD, even simpler and easier to use, working with states via the committee of chief ministers, constituted to share the best practices and take states along to encourage widespread adoption, provide greater incentives for adoption (discounts for digital transactions for fuel purchase), incentives for adoption (discounts for digital transactions for fuel purchase, railway tickets, highway tolls, insurance premiums, etc.) and on-ground mass-mobilization to train people to transact via digital modes. The entire district administration, common service centres (CSCs), e-Disha centres and post offices, and in some cases, even civil defence forces (in Jharkhand) are being mobilized to train people on digital modes. A 24-hour new TV channel, Digi Shala, has also been launched to explain step-by-step transaction methods in a simple way.

All this is showing early on-ground results—most digital payment modes have shown a rapid uptick (300 per cent to 1000 per cent) in the last month on a number of transactions on a per-day basis.

RBI has recently awarded payment bank licence to mobile operators. These telcos with their IT and digital capabilities, large consumer base and extensive distribution presence can transform the entire digital payment ecosystem in a short time. The country also needs a world-class all-pervasive Internet/broadband infrastructure which can provide secured and affordable services. It is also essential to push interoperability of Aadhaar devices, UPI, e-wallets and point of sale (POS) machines.

The benefits of this movement are immense—to both the consumer and economy at large. For the consumer, digitization enables seamless real-time tracking and on-spot payments, when compared with traditional modes like cheques which can be cumbersome and have protracted time spans for payments to be received. Digitization also enables easier recordkeeping—bill tracking and filing of tax returns can all be done in an easy and swift manner. Further digital transactions may yield tangible monetary benefits as well—recent incentives announced for fuel purchases, on insurance premiums, highway tolls, etc. make digital payments cheaper than transacting in cash! There is also the assurance of greater security—RBI-approved payment systems are amongst the most secure in the world—with reliable tracking and quick time alerts in case of exceptional withdrawals, etc.

India's economy also has multiplier benefits if payments go digital. The size of the formal economy grows, which directly augments tax revenues for the government. The amount of money available for social sector programmes increases, directly benefitting the common man. An additional benefit is that it enables the government to make taxes—both direct and indirect—more reasonable, again yielding tangible monetary benefits. Another direct beneficiary are banks, which have an increased pool of resources to lend to marginalized sections and provide credit to small businesses. In due course, credit history and data analytics will enable a higher level of financial inclusion.

Productivity of the economy also improves leakages and errors in resource distribution as we are already witnessing in the distribution of the Mahatma Gandhi National Rural Employment Guarantee Act (MGNREGA) and LPG subsidies. Elimination of ghost beneficiaries and DBT of subsidies to bank accounts have led to savings of ₹30,000 crore.

As Kenneth S. Rogoff in his fascinating book *The Curse of Cash* says, 'We are drowning in cash and its making us poorer and less safe. Paper money can also cripple monetary policy.' The cost of cash is high in India. Visa's report estimates India's cost of cash to be 1.7 per cent of the GDP annually. Turning less cash is expected to reduce this significantly high proportion by lower than 0.5 per cent. By going digital, banks and other financial institutions find their operating costs reduce to a minimum as cash handling is a major part of their daily activities operating expense.

Digitization of payments also has large-scale ramifications on legal compliance by third-party agencies, especially contractors. The enforcement of Minimum Wages Act is difficult if the wages are disbursed via cash. Mandating digital salary payments benefits workers greatly by ensuring that the workers get their rightful dues.

Finally, digitization also has an implication on public policy administration and enforcement. Recording transactions and payments provides scope for greater analysis and data-based policy framing. Digital payments are, thus, core to evidence-based policymaking.

Of course, as with any journey, there are risks—Indians, especially people with feature phones and those without phones, need to embrace digital payments technology. Initial signs are encouraging, but without sustained drive, usage rates might drop. Security is another key concern. All systems are subject to hacking and digital security onslaughts. Continued innovation is the only way to ensure that payment modes keep up with latest technology. Demonetization has been a radical move. It offers an immense opportunity to move from cash to digital payment transactions. We must embrace this change, and help transform India to a more formal, transparent and compliant country.

# Homegrown Innovation: How Start-ups are Transforming India

Technology and innovation are at the heart of transforming India. In recent years, technological change has been a major driver of rapid and sustained growth. An increasing number of advanced technology start-ups, the rising adoption of data analytics, AI and IoT in everyday processes, and continuing investor interest in Indian start-ups have helped create a dynamic innovation ecosystem in the country. A notable feature of India's start-up landscape is that the focus is not restricted to any single sector or group of the population. From providing access to financial services to enhancing the quality of health and education, India's start-ups are revolutionizing service delivery and quality across all segments of society.

India has certain inherent strengths that support the vibrant start-up culture. First, robust economic growth and a demographic dividend have created a large domestic consumer base with rising purchasing power. Second, a large number of STEM (science, technology, engineering and mathematics) graduates are eager to take part in India's technology revolution. Third, a large number of entrepreneurs are keen to address the opportunities and challenges that India offers. In addition, the government has focused on easing the business environment for start-ups, removing regulatory barriers for MSME and building infrastructural platforms to facilitate technology solutions. In this environment, more than USD 40 billion has poured into the Indian start-up ecosystem since 2014. The high level of investment in Indian start-ups emphasizes global and domestic investors' confidence in India's start-up ecosystem.

For example, take the financial services sector. The development of UPI—a real-time payment system that works across banks—has been a game changer. Together with initiatives like RuPay to support electronic payments, it has democratized access to finance for a large section of India's population. UPI, which was launched initially with 21 banks on board, today has 114 banks on the platform. It has crossed 400 million transactions in volume as of September 2018. In addition to enabling domestic start-ups to build payments solutions for India, it has incentivized large global technology companies such as Google, Amazon and Samsung to jump head first into the Indian payments markets. Other components of the financial services ecosystem have also bloomed. For example, technology-powered credit solutions have emerged as one of the most well-funded and rapidly growing segments in fintech in India, helping MSME realize their business potential.

## LEVERAGING TECHNOLOGY TO ENHANCE HEALTH AND EDUCATION

The focus on technology and Digital India has also enabled a new generation of socially focused start-ups that develop and scale solutions for sectors such as health, education and agriculture.

Healthcare in India faces the challenges of access, affordability and lack of quality practitioners and hospitals. Technology can help address these issues to a critical extent. SigTuple is addressing the issue of access through intelligent screening solutions aiding in quick diagnosis. It has developed a low-cost system for performing basic screening and advanced diagnosis of blood samples, X-rays and retinal scans. SigTuple's AI algorithms can analyse patient samples, send them to a pathologist for review and return final results to the point-of-care within five minutes. Tricog, another Indian start-up, uses AI for real-time cardiac diagnosis. Through its cloud-based electrocardiogram (ECG) machines installed at health centres, Tricog helps doctors detect heart complications faster than the conventional methods.

Similarly, within education, firms are using technology to address the lack of quality teachers, access to infrastructure as well as diverse pedagogical needs. For example, Embibe, which uses advanced AI for a personalized learning platform, is disrupting the education sector by improving learning outcomes at the individual student level. Embibe's 'relative quartile jump' methodology works on students' behaviour traits and sets goals for improving their behaviour. Using a smart test generation system combined with intelligent content ingestion, the platform generates learning paths and curves to improve students' learning and scoring capability.

## ENHANCING SERVICE DELIVERY AND EFFICIENCY OF PROCESSES THROUGH INNOVATION

Homegrown innovation has the potential to help India become a global leader in the Fourth Industrial Revolution. For example, a team from the Indian Institute of Technology (IIT), Madras, has developed an indigenous microprocessor called Shakti based on RISC-V architecture. The microprocessor has the potential to alter the face of computing. Developed at the Reconfigurable Intelligent Systems Engineering (RISE) Laboratory at IIT, Madras, RISC-V can process commands faster and in fewer cycles than the existing microprocessors. It can be a key catalyst in the Fourth Industrial Revolution by providing the infrastructural support for AI, robotics, 3D printing, and augmented and virtual reality.

Similarly, innovation has the potential to drive efficient outcomes across the existing sectors of the economy. India's agriculture sector is in imperative need of technology-enabled solutions that aid precision farming. SatSure, which has pioneered the use of big data analytics and machine learning in India's agriculture sector, uses a combination of satellite and weather data and information captured through IoT devices and drones to provide answers on crop volume, crop health, yield, and suggested harvesting dates. It recently developed an emergency flood portal for Kerala floods and built models for crop damage due to Cyclone Titli in Srikakulam, Andhra Pradesh, for mid-season calamity crop insurance payments. Another AgriTech company, Vasar Labs uses AI and IoT to develop water management and agriculture advisory services. It uses satellite-based data, weather advisory, soil moisture data and other IoT sensors to predict the amount of water needed for normal yields, date of sowing advisory, pest and diseases forecast, and crop acreage estimates.

Another start-up, Haptik, has built one of the world's largest conversational AI platforms. Haptik is a 24x7 chat-based personal assistant. For instance, one can book a cab or flight tickets, recharge phones, pay utility bills, or web check-in for a flight though the app. It now reaches over 100 million devices each month. The company has processed over a billion interactions till date and helps firms leverage the power of AI to automate critical business processes and improve the overall customer experience.

## TECHNOLOGY AND INCLUSIVE GROWTH

Given our rapid progress in the start-up space and positive growth trajectory of technology start-ups, India is fast becoming a hub for the application of frontier technologies across sectors, globally. Indian start-ups are continuously finding innovative technological solutions in health, education, financial services, industry and agriculture. These solutions do not restrict their focus to 1.3 billion Indians but they bring benefits for the global citizens who will be moving from poverty to middle class and from rural to urban areas in the coming decade.

For India to continue leveraging technology as a mechanism of sustained growth, we need to continue strengthening our innovation ecosystem and nurturing start-ups. We have already taken massive steps in building enabling infrastructure, supporting institutions and regulatory environment that will allow start-ups to thrive. Going forward, we need to ensure that we continue supporting innovation to deliver inclusive growth.

# Time for Revolutionary Changes to Ensure that the IBC Provides Swift Resolution

The Insolvency and Bankruptcy Code (IBC), 2016, is a deep, structural reform that replaced a highly fragmented insolvency law framework in India which was mired with delays and misuse. The insolvency reform has been attempted in India since 1993, but multiple attempts were abortive, causing insolvency resolution to take decades, thus tying up precious bank capital and crowding out fresh lending. The IBC marks a clear shift, representing a comprehensive structural reform, rather than minor tinkering.

It was intended to ensure the speedy redistribution of assets and businesses that otherwise would languish in long-drawn court processes and red tape, and would instead fall prey to the processes that India's courts have traditionally been victims of. Pendency, indiscriminate delays and an erosion of the intent of the IBC have startled investor confidence. Increasingly, loopholes have been found and deviations sought, which extend the statutorily prescribed time limits for resolution, and therefore shake the foundations on which this landmark legislative reform has been passed. It envisages a ceiling of 180 days, extendable at most to 270 days. Notable cases such as the Essar Steel matter have made a mockery of these timelines. At nearly 675 days or 22 months, and at a cost to banks/lenders of ₹17 crore each day, the Essar Steel matter has become the torchbearer for hurting the credibility of what is universally accepted as a world-leading reform.

There is no ambiguity about the jurisdiction or validity of the IBC, and the Supreme Court of India in January upheld the constitutional validity of the law. Justices R. Nariman and N. Sinha, when dismissing several petitions challenging the IBC, settled the matter once and for all by declaring that it is good law and enforceable. Further, in the other judgements of the Supreme Court, it has been held that the commercial wisdom of the Committee of Creditors cannot be interfered with judicially. The Supreme Court has unequivocally stated that there is no provision for the tribunals to interfere with the commercial decision of the Committee of Creditors. The Bankruptcy Law Reform Committee (headed by Sri T.K. Vishwanathan), which provided the intellectual nucleus of the IBC, as well as its first draft, in its report envisaged the resolution plan being approved on commercial grounds by the Committee of Creditors and provided certain safeguards for operational and dissenting creditors. These safeguards are in line with the UN Commission on International Trade Law (UNCITRAL) Legislative Guide as well as the World Bank Ease of Business parameters to prevent holdouts. So long as such safeguards are met, the tribunal is not required to intervene, or manifest any violation of law or process.

The National Company Law Tribunal (NCLT) has been interfering in matters relating to the share of operational and financial creditors and the manner in which it should be shared—indeed purely commercial matters. This is contrary to the intent and philosophy of the law. It is also resulting in interminable delays and is draining bank funds further.

Recent estimates peg losses to banks' income at approximately ₹4,000 crore, primarily due to pendency in the resolution of the original 12 major insolvency cases that the RBI had referred to last year. Referred in June 2017, just four of the matters have been resolved, with the others having been before the NCLT for almost double the prescribed ceiling, or in excess of 470 days. There's more—approximately 30 per cent of more than 800 ongoing Corporate Insolvency Resolution Process have surpassed the time ceiling statutorily prescribed, with an additional 20 per cent having crossed the six-month timeline as per a recent study. Therefore, the procedural and process delays, if anything, are only causing additional depreciation of assets.

It is imperative that adjournments or procedural loopholes do not cause the IBC to become a less efficient mechanism. To attract global participation in India's economy, the resolution process must be timely, and not thrown into disarray that undermines credibility and resolve. Some suggestions that could lead to righting the course are needed.

A systematic and rigorous mechanism to exponentially enhance capacity must be immediately undertaken so that the number of benches can be expanded to ensure no matter is unresolved, delayed, or turned down. The capacity of the NCLT is an issue, and the numbers of matters that are admitted far outweigh the existing capacity. A specialized bench of the NCLT to handle only IBC matter would be essential, as this would engender depth and specialization. Evidence from

China suggests that this could significantly reduce time for resolution as well as improve access to credit. The physical infrastructure of the NCLT must be bolstered and they must be provided with technological support for case management, prediction and disposal.

Meanwhile, a lot of groundwork has been done on making palatable prepackaged resolution solutions, led by the Ministry of Corporate Affairs (MCA) and the Insolvency and Bankruptcy Board of India (IBBI). These should be further expanded so as to ensure that due diligence is observed and solutions have been debated and more or less agreed upon prior to admission before the NCLT, with appropriate safeguards against holdouts. Like in the UK, a 'prepack pool', which is an independent body of experienced professionals, may also be considered to be set up which will provide expert opinion and recommendations regarding prepacked deals. Such recommendations could be factored in by the parties and Tribunal in the final decision-making.

At the same time, one radical idea could be to make the National Company Law Appellate Tribunal the final word on resolution with a directive from the Supreme Court stating that no bonafide resolution may be challenged before any high court or the Supreme Court except in cases of malafide circumstances, such as fraud. Essentially, this will act as being double jeopardy against potential litigators who have been unsuccessful in the resolution, but want another shot at taking over a distressed company. A process could be considered whereby any causes of action in civil matters against a company going for resolution must be adjudicated before it is admitted to the NCLT under the IBC. Alternatively, as provided in the IBC and the regulations under it, such claims could be accounted for as 'contingent liabilities' under the resolution plan and it can be voted for and approved on this basis. This way, all causes of action must be extinguished or resolved before the 270-day timeline kicks in or will otherwise be addressed subsequently. Equally important is a two-pronged due diligence signed off by the resolution professional fully trained in the process. A prevailing concern is a mismatch between what a winning bidder expects to receive and the actual state of play due to leakages or missing assets during the process. The dual prong could essentially put a stop to mismatches and any dichotomy.

There is no doubt whatsoever that the IBC has been a boon. Loan defaults in excess of ₹1.2 lakh crore have been resolved just because the IBC exists, prior even to them being admitted. Of more than the 9,000 cases that approached the NCLT for initiation of insolvency proceedings, 4,400 cases have already been disposed of, with nearly 85 per cent of the cases, or more than 3,500 cases, being resolved pre-admission. It is, therefore, clear that the IBC, when enforced and enabled in accordance with legislative intent, is an unprecedented reform, acting as much a deterrent for lags and delays as an actual cure for a previously unsolved problem.

A reform like the IBC, no matter how revolutionary it may be, is only as good as its implementation allows it to be. Adhering to time limits is sacrosanct. If it takes revolutionary measures to ensure the IBC is implemented as per its intent and ability, then now is the time to do so. We cannot afford any more delays in the resolution process.

# How to Break into the Top 50: Enhance Jobs and GDP Growth by Further Improving Ease of Doing Business and Slashing Red Tape

In his very first interaction with the Secretaries of the Government of India, Prime Minister Narendra Modi had expressed his deep anguish at India's poor performance in World Bank's Ease of Doing Business index. His view was that India had made itself a highly complex, difficult and complicated place to conduct business in and it was necessary for rules, regulations and procedures built over the years to be dismantled so that India could become an easy and simple place for investors.

In his view, it was necessary for the government to act as a facilitator and catalyst and create an environment where private sector could create wealth. The Prime Minister felt that India needed to improve its rank for its own sake and not for World Bank's sake.

In the past three years, this work has been undertaken with single-minded pursuit, structural reforms have been vigorously driven, procedures have been simplified, rules have been modified and almost 1,200 laws have been abolished. The measures put together have been unprecedented.

In the last three years, India's position in the World Bank's Ease of Doing Business index has jumped up from 142 to 100—a jump of 42 positions. The World Bank's ranking is important as it is widely publicized and plays a significant role in the positioning and branding of a nation.

India is a large country, bigger than 24 countries of Europe. Much of the action relating to investments has shifted to its states. Therefore, it is necessary that we make it easy and simple for businesses to be conducted in the states of India. The government has initiated competition amongst the states and the UTs on defined outcomes of the Ease of Doing Business index.

There has been heavy competition. In the first year, Gujarat was number one. In the second year, Telangana and Andhra Pradesh beat Gujarat for the first spot. The best thing was that the mineral-rich states of Jharkhand and Chhattisgarh competed heavily and came fourth and fifth, respectively.

Competition amongst states has now become intense. The process of ranking the states is clearly working. Since ranking is being put in the public domain, there is heavy pressure on Chief Ministers and State bureaucracy to perform and deliver. Clearly, good governance has now become good politics.

Learning from the example of the Ease of Doing Business index, NITI Aayog has carried this principle forward for state rankings on defined outcomes in the field of health, education and composite water management. While we have challenged the states, we are also partnering them to radically improve their performance before ranks are announced. This in many ways has been a unique experience of competitive federalism.

The World Bank's Doing Business 2018 report recognizes India as one of the top reformers that year. While India's rank has improved in six of the 10 indicators, distance to the frontier has improved on nine out of 10 indicators, showing that India's reforms are contributing to bridging the gap with the best in the world in almost all indicators. The distance to the frontier score here means the distance of the Indian economy to the frontier country/countries which rank as the best performers in the particular indicators across all ranked economies. India ranks in the top five in the world when it comes to protecting minority investors and ranks in the top 30 in the world with regard to three indicators—protecting minority investors, receiving credit and getting electricity. The report has appreciated reforms across sectors, from streamlining processes, reducing permits to cutting time and costs.

The fact that India has made a substantial jump of 30 ranks is extremely noteworthy as it is very rare and difficult for large countries to make such a quantum jump. A jump of 30 ranks has rarely been seen before. However, India needs to radically improve in dealing with construction permits where it ranks at 181, enforcement of contracts where it is ranked at 164, starting a business where it is at 156, trading across border where it is at 146 and registering property where it is still at 154.

What does India need to do to improve its position in these parameters and break into top 50 in the next two years?

In registering property, the critical challenge is that records related to land are spread across many departments, Sub Registrars office, land records, banks for mortgages and courts in cases of disputes. This means that a buyer must visit every single department separately to find the records. Therefore, reducing the search time will require massive digitization at various offices and linking records together, using a unique ID.

In enforcement of contracts, the establishment of dedicated commercial courts at the district-court level in Delhi and Mumbai can go a long way towards reducing the time taken for restoring commercial disputes. These courts should also introduce online electronic case management systems and should rigorously abide by the civil procedure code limit of a maximum of three adjournments per case.

Despite important reforms in starting a business, India continues to be ranked poorly because other countries have reformed faster. India's rank can benefit from further integrating registration processes into single form by converging GST with PAN/TAN registration, integrating the Employees' Provident Fund Organization and Employees' State Insurance Corporation along with shops and establishment registration processes. It also needs business process re-engineering to reduce the propensity to inspect by switching to real-time registration and a culture of risk-based verifications. This requires cutting layers of bureaucracy.

When it comes to trading across borders, India has implemented far-reaching reforms but the private sector feedback seems to indicate that the impact is still to be felt. We need to do extensive process re-engineering to ensure that all approving authorities in the customs-clearance process deliver seamless online approvals and bring shipping lines on board to deliver timely online service.

While reforms in dealing with construction permits have been acknowledged, there is scope for greater improvement. Further reforms require integration of central and state governments' NOC (No Objection Certificate) departments with the Municipal Corporation, single windows to ensure online approvals and service delivery, using GIS to provide transparent and conclusive information on permissions required and risk-based principles to reduce the number of inspection and approvals.

Lastly, we need to train the staff in all our departments so that they become champions of reforms and can provide correct advice to applicants.

India must continue to accelerate the momentum of reforms in the coming years. It has demonstrated the political will for structural reforms and the ability to converge and integrate across departments. Providing greater vigour, energy and dynamism to this movement will enable India to definitely break into the top 50 in the next two years.

There will be many challenges. Bureaucracy must continue to be an active agent of process re-engineering, hard reforms must be pushed vigorously, administrative blocks must be eliminated and silos have to be broken down. India's ambition must be to become the easiest and simplest place for investors to do business in.

# The Age of Disruption and The Future of Jobs: Why We Must Embrace the New Era of Artificial Intelligence, Blockchain and Robots

The ancient Chinese game GO, which has a very high number of possible moves, was considered almost impossible for a computer to beat humans two years ago. Last year when Alpha GO (a GO programme designed by two GO players) beat the best human professional, GO Player Lee Sedol, in a five-game match, by learning from millions of games, it became clear that machine learning has breached even the bastion of strategic thought. Impossible Foods, a Fourth Industrial Revolution technology company, makes plant-based food that smells, tastes and looks like real meat. It threatens the future of the $90 billion meat industry. If only 20 per cent of the world's population switches from eating real meat to alternative proteins, it would free up 12 per cent of total freshwater and 400 million hectares of land, and reduce 960 megatons of $CO_2$ emission. Both traditional manufacturing and service-oriented industries are being disrupted in a manner we have never seen before.

We are in the midst of the fourth wave of technological advancement—the phenomenal use of new digital industrial technologies known as the Fourth Industrial Revolution. The word 'revolution' implies abrupt and radical change. The first Industrial Revolution spanned from around mid-1700 to 1840, triggered by the invention of the steam engine which led to mechanical production. The second Industrial Revolution made mass production feasible and was catalyzed by the discovery of electricity and assembly line. This began in late nineteenth century and continued till early twentieth century. The third Industrial Revolution began in the 1960s and was driven by computers, digital technology and the Internet. The fourth Industrial Revolution is being driven by ten technologies that are transforming industrial production. These are: autonomous robots; simulation; big data and analytics; augmented reality; the cloud; cybersecurity; additive manufacturing; horizontal and vertical integration; and IoT and AI. These technologies are impacting the entire production value chain, from design and productivity, to speed and quality of production.

There is widespread concern on the potential impact of the Fourth Industrial Revolution on employment. A vast range of jobs are at risk of extinction and rapid scaling could lead to accumulation of job losses. The other fear is that new technologies would lead to increase in inequalities and lack of social cohesion. Elon Musk has stated that AI represents an essential threat to humanity and has suggested tight regulations. Bill Gates has stated that robots need to be taxed to compensate for greater efficiency compared to humans and suggested that the pace of automation should be slowed down.

A McKinsey Global Institute report, 'Jobs Lost, Jobs Gained: Workforce Transitions in A Time of Automation,' estimates that between 400 million and 800 million people around the globe could be displaced by automation and will need to find new jobs by 2030. While new jobs will be available, people will require new skills to find new jobs. There will be considerable need for re-skilling and training.

Let us look at what new technologies could do to enable India to technologically leapfrog. The two indicators holding India back in Ease of Doing Business are enforcement of contracts where India is 164 out of 190 countries and registering property where India is 154 out of 190. They account for India's overall poor ranking and have acted as a major barrier for investors to India. About 3 crore cases are currently pending in various courts of India. These include 44.5 lakh cases in high courts and 2.6 crore lower court cases. Two-thirds of all civil cases in district courts relate to registering land. Blockchain-based smart contracts could radically reduce litigation, bring transparency in land registry and eliminate corruption relating to land. India has a billion biometrics on Aadhaar. We have a unique opportunity to leverage our public identities to have many applications on a blockchain network.

According to a PwC report, AI will contribute as much as 15.7 trillion to the world economy by 2030. This is more than the combined output of China and India. Given India's strength in technology, favourable demographics and structural advantages in availability of advanced data, India can be a pioneer in the field of AI. AI has the potential to add US $957 billion or 15 per cent of current gross value added to India's economy by 2035 (Accenture Report). India's data diversity is a big draw for global AI implementers as data is the fuel that powers current generation AI algorithms utilizing deep learning. AI can be a game changer in government where 'scale' and 'quality' need to be addressed simultaneously.

Robots and AI together can double productivity every four years compared to 10 years that humans take working on their own. Even simple robots are increasing productivity by 15-20 per cent in China. Foxconn has replaced 60,000 workers in factories with robots. Robotics industry-spending is set to exceed $135 billion in 2019, nearly double its 2015 figure. Robots would increase productivity, decrease costs and relieve humans from difficult and discomforting jobs.

What does India need to do to embrace technology, create new jobs and meet the requirements of the changed scenario?

Firstly, we must realign India's education system to emphasize skills rather than mere degrees. We must move away from the Anglo-Saxon system of education with emphasis on academic degrees to hands-on learning in practical subjects. A beginning has already been made by AIM. By 2018 end, nearly 2000 schools will have ATLs with robots, 3D printers, additive machinery, IoT and mentors so that children from class VI onwards can build and experiment rather than only imbibe. It is the first programme of this size and scale globally which aims to change the fundamentals of our education system to better enable our society to work in the future.

Secondly, we must constantly upgrade skills for newer and higher-paid jobs. There is a severe shortage of skilled manpower. India needs massive upgradation programmes in new technologies. Our IITs and International Institutes of Information Technology must redefine themselves as institutes driving cutting-edge technologies for the Fourth Industrial Revolution.

Thirdly, we must create a highly flexible, resilient and adaptive workforce which is multi-skilled and has the capacity to undertake digital tasks from anywhere rather than a fixed location.

Fourthly, we must initiate measures to ensure that India's citizens and its workforce are fully prepared to embrace the new era of AI, blockchain, additive manufacturing and emerging technologies. India cannot afford to bypass this revolution. This requires a new mindset. Our policies must drive this change.

Fifthly, we must work across disciplines and institutional boundaries. We must break silos. Medical data is an example. Life-saving opportunities can be utilized by sharing large sets of genomic data across different health providers and research organizations.

Sixthly, our focus must be on the social sector—education, health and nutrition—where new technologies will enable us to leapfrog, improve the quality of life and enhance our human development index. These are also the sectors where maximum jobs will be created.

Countries are still navigating the early stages of transformation of this new industrial revolution. Can India jumpstart this transformation?

# Unlocking Indian Heritage's Economic Potential

India, with several millennia's history, boasts of a diverse and rich heritage. Each region of our subcontinent, without exception, boasts of monumental buildings and remarkable archaeology. Yet, less than 15,000 monuments and heritage structures are legally protected in India—a fraction of the 600,000 protected in the UK.

Even those structures which are considered to be of national/state or local importance in India and protected as such remain under threat from urban pressures, neglect, vandalism and worse, demolition, only for the value of the land they stand upon. This poor state of preservation of a large part of our national heritage is a result of the inability of those entrusted with their management to unlock the economic potential of these sites and demonstrate that conservation effort can lead to meeting development objectives in the most sustainable manner.

The first step towards this would be to ensure that visits to monuments and archaeological sites are exciting for both local residents and international visitors. Following decades of effort, we, in India, boast of several thousand sites, contemporary and even grander to the well-known Mohenjo Daro and Harappa. India has 34 UNESCO-designated World Heritage Sites—only a handful of countries have more. Lack of effective management and presentation, however, results in most archaeological sites being inaccessible to the general public or not being richly experienced. It is required, even for sites such as the Taj Mahal, that the cultural context and intangible heritage—music, food, ritual, dress, personalities, festivals—associated with the sites is explained to the visitor. Cultural events that would usually attract large numbers should be organized at lesser-visited monuments and heritage enthusiasts should be encouraged to buy annual passes that allow unlimited visits. Funds spent on introducing such measures and facilities will quickly yield rich dividends.

In some states, notably Rajasthan and Telangana, efforts have been made to encourage 'adoption' of monuments for their management and maintenance. If we are to pass on to future generations our heritage in a better condition than what we inherited it in, there needs to be liberalization in the cultural sector and responsibility should be entrusted to private entities, schools and universities, non-profits, and resident welfare associations. Responsibilities can go beyond maintenance and cleanliness with non-governmental partners engaging the specialists required and the government agencies supervising the effort to ensure that highest standards of conservation are achieved for these irreplaceable assets. With CSR (corporate social responsibility) funds entitled to be spent for conservation, finding required funds should be possible.

Heritage buildings everywhere utilize local materials and local communities hold the traditional knowledge to work with these locally available materials. Obviously, any conservation effort then has to source locally, creating employment and economic opportunities. Many Indian Maharajas commissioned forts, palaces and temples in times of drought as a lifesaving economic incentive for the populace. 'Make in India' objectives will thus be met by any well-planned and implemented conservation effort while simultaneously creating an economic asset that continues to pay rich dividends for years to come.

Only a limited number of heritage buildings are tourist attractions. For the rest, new functions need to be incentivized and planned. Most of the 600,000 protected heritage structures in the UK are in private management and as historic buildings are considered better built, they command high premium.

Adaptive reuse of heritage buildings in Europe has ensured that several churches—fallen into disuse—have been converted into unique experiential tourism. We need to incentivize private conservation and preservation works. Property tax waiver, permission for change of land use and transferable development rights are amongst other incentives owners of heritage buildings or those residing within the 100-m 'prohibited zones' of nationally protected monuments could be receiving. Besides use as hotels or museums or libraries, heritage buildings or monuments could also easily be adapted to serve as schools, lending economic value to the local communities. It is always cheaper and easier to convert a building than build afresh, while also representing a higher aesthetic and building quality.

To be meaningful, conservation works at our national and local heritage sites should go beyond the fences erected around these sites by the British in the nineteenth and twentieth centuries. Conservation works need to be coupled with urban improvements, improved transport infrastructure, providing economic opportunities, improving health, education and sanitation infrastructure. Only then will the heritage assets be valued by those inhabiting around them. Conservationists have often expected local communities to contribute towards conservation effort while not offering any incentives and imposing heavy restrictions; such an approach is never likely to succeed.

One of the world's most frequently cited conservation success stories has resulted from the non-profit partnership established by the Aga Khan Trust for Culture with the Archaeological Survey of India, Central Public Works Department and the South Delhi Municipal Corporation in the Humayun's Tomb, in the Nizamuddin area of Delhi. Here, over a ten-year period, conservation works have been undertaken on over 40 structures, leading to a tenfold increase in visitor numbers and a two-fold expansion of the World Heritage Site to include 11 monuments in addition to Humayun's Tomb. The Aga Khan Trust for Culture has assisted the Archaeological Survey of India to take ownership of an additional 35 acres of land—freeing it from encroachment and implemented landscape restoration at these monuments—by planting over 10,000 trees in the process. As conservation work requires 500,000 days of work for craftsmen, a strong case has been made for making conservation work eligible for MGNREGA funds.

As a result of this partnership project, over 20,000 inhabiting the adjoining Nizamuddin Basti today have an improved quality of life resulting from street improvements, landscaping of neighbourhood parks, building of community toilet complexes, improved primary education and providing health facilities that have been used by over 400,000 from citywide location. Emphasis of the Sufi cultural legacy through cultural performances and exhibitions has also instilled a sense of pride in the local community. These efforts have a significant economic impact—locally and citywide. Providing appropriate vocational training has meant thousands of jobs and economic opportunities, for example, selling of souvenirs crafted by the women in Nizamuddin.

The successful implementation of this urban conservation and development effort has resulted from corporates, national and international trusts, government agencies, public sector entities, academic institutes partnering the Aga Khan Trust for Culture in this effort. With limited human resources available to government entities mandated to implement urban improvement and conservation projects in our historic city centres, similar partnerships need to be established. Just as anywhere else in the world, our heritage can be leveraged for economic gain through tourism earnings as well as opportunities for craftsmen and local communities.

# Limitless Possibilities for the Unmanned Aircraft Systems Industry

Rapid advancements in technologies have resulted in a paradigm shift in aviation brought on by the advent of the Unmanned Aircraft Systems (UAS) in not only the airspace but also in the business arena. Innovative UAS-enabled solutions in areas as diverse as the military, civil and commercial sector are rapidly growing. Today, anyone can fly a drone with a little investment and some basic understanding of technology.

UAS typically fall into one of four functional categories, although multi-role airframe platforms are becoming more prevalent. The first functional category includes military applications such as their employment as target and decoys and missions that include reconnaissance and surveillance, combat roles such as loitering missiles, communications and logistics.

The second functional category includes civil applications, which are those involving non-defence government agencies pertaining to nearly every aspect of smart governance, law enforcement, anti-terrorism, geo-mapping, fisheries and forest management, disaster management, event monitoring, environmental control and monitoring (including air and sea pollution), telecommunications, crop monitoring mineral exploration, ground mapping and photography, meteorological observation, 3-D modeling and digital elevation mapping, and critical infrastructure protection. Vitally, track surveys of railways can be conducted to prevent railway accidents either due to sabotage or defects. Potentially, UAS-aided crop surveys, pesticides and fertilizer spraying, health of water reservoirs, and irrigation can transform the lives and livelihoods of farmers.

The third functional category is Commercial Unmanned Aerial Vehicles (UAVs) applications, which includes grid and gas pipelines surveys, mining, logistics, agriculture, mapping soil conditions and crop growth, oil and gas exploration, and media coverage. They can even help in healthcare, transporting human organs at short notice and offer several opportunities for innovation in the 'way of doing business'.

Finally, we have UAVs specifically designed for research and development such as meteorology, avalanche studies and socio-economic data collection.

It is therefore no surprise that no other industry has transformed from military hardware to mass application as quickly as drones. In India, like most other countries, the UAVs started off from being used for defence purposes, but are now increasingly used in the civilian, commercial and the recreational space. Development in fields of automation, robotics, miniaturization, materials science, thermal imaging, etc. have enabled diverse civilian and commercial application of drones in sectors like agriculture, power, infrastructure, mining and telecom to undertake various activities with significant improvements in efficiency and cost. Consequently, the global UAS industry has steadily attracted the attention of operators, manufacturers and investors alike.

The drone industry is likely to go the way of the automobile industry with spillover applications in the industrial sector and in the consumer market too. This is for a variety of reasons. On the one hand its transformational impact on ease of doing business, the way of doing business and the cost of doing business is driving the growth of the industry and, on the other, regulations and concerns of the widespread and indiscriminate use of the technology raises valid security, safety and privacy concerns. The Government recognizes this duality and has to carefully prepare the ground for the early induction of this technology into India. Integrating the UAVs into civilian air space is a challenging job and requires an appropriate regulatory framework for operations. Several countries such as Australia, Canada, Japan, Malaysia, Singapore, UK and US have promulgated guidelines for the operation of mini UAS, generally limited by weight (20 kg), by altitude (300 ft) and operating range (limited to line of sight). It is hugely important for India to facilitate and promote the energetic development of the UAS industry in India and strive to secure a global leadership in this sunrise technology and aspire to become a global manufacturing hub in times to come.

Hence this opportunity comes with its share of challenges, which can broadly be categorized as individual rights concerns and collective security and safety concerns and therefore a need for regulation.

Whilst in the military sector the regulations and compliances are resolved, the civil and commercial sectors are still faced with obstacles for its growth. Foremost amongst them is the lack of a regulatory regime for the UAS operations.

Despite the obvious promise of UAV technology and its direct impact on better governance, socio-economic development, fillip to domestic manufacturing, potential for generation of diverse high-level skills, and provision for assorted 'smart' services to name a few, the regulatory framework is awaiting promulgation. I hope the final format of the regulatory regime would unequivocally support the growth of the UAS industry for a variety of security, social and economic benefits for the nation.

For India and its industry leaders, it is imperative that they use this period to develop their business plans and identify the niche areas where their interest lies.

Currently, the main user of UAS is the armed forces. The first application of UAVs was as targets and decoys in the early 1990s and the first drone was operated in 1996. In the past few years, the demand for various types of UAS has grown exponentially. In the civilian space, some police forces at the state level have been operating micro-UAS. In the commercial space there is a sizeable demand from Power Grid/GAIL/ONGC for grid and pipeline survey, Bollywood, agriculture and mining, construction sites, telecom towers, and geo-physical surveys amongst others. UAS can transform the efficiency of this service exponentially. There is also increasing demand for drones for recreational purpose. There is thus a tremendous opportunity for the business community and the UAS to expand its user base, which can also be an efficient tool in the hands of the Government for its various programme requirements.

Widespread adoption of the UAS through a facilitative framework would be a transformational step from ease of doing business to a better way of doing business for the government and citizens. Adequate demand exists to build a UAS manufacturing and services ecosystem in India.

So far, as the UAV industry in India is concerned, a few pointers are important. First the import of drones is prohibited, its manufacture requires an industrial licence, and its operations have not been regularized.

In this context it is commendable that national industrial capability for UAS has been developed to a reasonable level of sophistication. In India today, there is some design and engineering capability in the private sector whilst the DRDO and National Aeronautical Laboratory (NAL) have designed targets and drones; but the high-end systems are on the drawing board and are at the testing and trial stages. COTS software for automatic take-off and landing and automatic flight control system is available. There is also some capability in system integration including ground control stations but limited to mini UAS in the private sector. Aerostructure manufacturing expertise is limited to secondary structures, and gaps exist in manufacture of undercarriage, primary structures, etc. There is no national capability for manufacture of propulsion package engines, systems and high-end payloads and this is an area where investment to develop a national capability is warranted.

Apart from the basic system there would also be demand for a variety of sub-systems such as aero engines, diverse types of payloads, avionics and communication equipment, various types of computer hardware such as processors, displays and man-machine interface and, at lower tiers of the manufacturing process, transistors, amplifiers and PCBs too. The potential is enormous for the growth of the indigenous electronic sector and software industry also.

I see a second line of business in the UAS segment. That is of being a service provider offering the UAS for the entire spectrum of remote sensing, surveillance, monitoring, estimation road/rail construction projects along new alignments, for open cast mining, landfills and dumping ground waste volume calculation and disposal study, for landslides and avalanche studies and many more such applications. This would require investors to own several hundreds of UAS systems and then lease them to operators for undertaking various sub tasks, analysis, etc. This in effect would be quite like the Uber and Ola models. This is a transformational market for start-ups and entrepreneurs who are presently constrained by the lack of clarity on the use of UAS for commercial applications. In the UAS services sector, the main chunk of the business would be in surveys and monitoring; MRO, upgrades and life extensions services; logistics and communication services; training; and design and engineering. Additional business opportunities that would be generated in the UAS industry as a whole include two key areas: air traffic management systems for drone traffic, and anti-drone systems. As the industry grows, it is vitally important to simultaneously bring in a comprehensive ecosystem for the safe operation of drones and provide Unmanned Traffic Management (UTM) solutions. This is a sector with substantial challenges and opportunities where Indian software engineers can contribute. With regard to anti-drone systems, a new technology industry is on the rise in response to fears over malicious use of drones by terrorists, enemy forces or even deliberate incursions into privacy. Anti-drone technology is rapidly evolving and offers an opportunity for Indian engineers.

In conclusion, it has been said that drones are going to

replace 80 per cent of operations presently carried out by manned aircrafts. The business opportunity is tremendous and if unleashed has the potential to transform many of the sectors and modernize India rapidly.

The Indian market for UAS is of the order of about US $50 billion over the next 15 years. India must realize the full potential of this technology and leverage it to its best advantage as a powerful tool not only for security and safety, good governance, increased productivity but also to encourage consumer and commercial applications to develop a sophisticated UAS industry sector and make a New India.

In this regard I would like to make a few recommendations to energize the domestic UAS industry.

The Armed Forces, being the largest customer for UAS, offers the best prospect for kick-starting the UAS industry in India. However, piecemeal imports to meet individual service demands must be discontinued for the indigenous UAS industry to grow and demand aggregation to create the critical mass for viable commercial investments could be considered. This aggregation would include the requirements of the security forces under MHA, railways etc.

India should aspire to be the global hub for design, development and manufacture of aero-engines and aero-structures for all types of UAS. The payloads and avionics space are already crowded with many suppliers. Basis the demand aggregation for engines, it would potentially offer a sizeable market for overseas investors, provided the scale and size of the opportunity are adequately quantified.

The regulatory framework for opening up UAS operations for civil and commercial services should be promulgated early in line with global best practices. This should include requirements of a UAS traffic management system and anti-drone systems.

One of the primary beneficiaries of UAS would be the agriculture, fisheries, forests and irrigation sector. UAS services by start-ups must be encouraged through incentives, benefits, tax breaks, etc. for such services will be for the benefit of the agriculture sector.

Finally, drones provide better information awareness—whether for governance, commerce or security. In times to come, I am certain that this technology will open new vistas of business and further accentuate the growth of the industry.

THREE

# SOCIAL TRANSFORMATION

# Catalyzing Rapid Social Change: The Key to India's Growth with Equity

With the election phase not long gone, it's important take a step back to maintain a clear line of vision on what eventually is of key importance—the ease of living and access to satisfaction of our citizens, from the grass roots upwards. A series of structural reforms have transformed India's social sector. This is critical, given the volume and magnitude of this sector. One of India's biggest challenges has been, and continues to be, the state of our social capital. The systematic modus operandi has been to move away from a macro policy, and instead to immerse with the grass-roots needs, leveraging massive advances in e-governance and information and communication technology (ICT) tools to become real-time in reform and involving communities' own investment in their development.

## ADVANCES IN NUTRITION

Nutrition has traditionally been left ignored despite the daunting challenges we face. As per NFHS (National Family Health Survey)-4, nearly one in every three child is stunted and every other woman is anaemic. Taking into account the multiple determinants of malnutrition, the recently launched POSHAN (PM's Overarching Scheme for Holistic Nourishment) Abhiyaan is an overarching umbrella scheme that brings together a comprehensive package of intervention and services focused on the vital 1000 days of a child's life delivered by multiple ministries through an appropriate governance structure that fosters sectoral convergence. POSHAN Abhiyaan further ideates a Jan Andolan through involvement of local communities to push for a social and behaviour change communication (SBCC), since focusing merely on the supply side without convincing families of the need to avail of the required services would understandably yield diminishing returns to government investments. The Pradhan Mantri Matru Vandana Yojana (PMMVY) is a conditional cash transfer scheme for pregnant mothers and lactating women that would reinforce the SBCC strategy. The beneficiary cost norms of the supplementary nutrition programme under the Integrated Child Development Services has been revised substantially upwards, and indexed to inflation so that the entitlement in real terms remains impactful. Mission Indradhanush has ensured that in the lowest-quintile 201 districts, full immunization coverage rates have increased by well over 10 times. The relentless focus on hygiene and sanitation through the SBM has increased sanitation coverage in rural India from 39 per cent (October 2014) to well over 95 per cent, therefore saving lives.

## HEALTHCARE REVOLUTION—AYUSHMAN BHARAT

Major work has been done in the health sector. Firstly, groundbreaking work has happened in preventive and primary care. The goal of establishing 1.5 lakh well-equipped and appropriately resourced health and wellness centres that offer comprehensive primary care with free drugs and diagnostic facilities is well and truly on its way, with 15,000 already established. Syncing health with healthy lifestyles is a key priority here.

The landmark Ayushman Bharat scheme has transformed India's healthcare. In just 200 days, 20 lakh patients have received insurance treatment worth more than ₹2,600 crore, along with more than 3 crore e-cards having been generated. These are staggering figures.

## INVESTING IN OUR FUTURE THROUGH EDUCATION

Providing high-quality education remains a mammoth task and an ongoing challenge. An E&Y study on higher education points out that, by 2030, India will be the youngest country in the world, with 14 crore individuals in the college-going age group. World-class education, especially higher education, remains one of our biggest challenges.

There have been key outcomes in the sector. Categorization of universities for graded autonomy has been initiated with well-performing universities (i.e. those receiving accreditation score above specified benchmarks) to be awarded various dimensions of academic, administrative and financial autonomy. Another outcome is the strengthening of accreditation framework which enables additional accreditation agencies to be empaneled by a credible and independent Accreditation Advisory Council (AAC). All accreditation reports must therefore be made public online for transparency. Further, display of accreditation grade/ unaccredited status must be made mandatory on institutions' websites and all public information material. A third reform is the enabling of online degree programmes, permitting universities awarded with the highest accreditation grade to offer online degree programmes. A fourth reform allows the check on quality of journals notified by the University Grants Commission (UGC). In order to remove spurious journals, UGC was directed to review the list of journals notified by it to award points to faculty for publications.

In schools, states have successfully synchronized academic initiatives with administrative reforms that create an enabling environment for these new practices to take root, aided by technology for learning outcomes and monitoring/evaluation. The focus has been on systems approach towards improving learning outcomes. These are being replicated by all states. NITI has also developed the state-level School Education Quality index which seeks to make improvements in learning outcomes a focal point of governance by ranking states and putting them in the public domain.

A lot of work is happening on introducing innovation to education through ICT so as to reach the farthest corners of India, and this sector is key for growth in the next 10 years. A unique example is of Banka District of Bihar which has utilized mobile telephony to spread education in schools.

## THE ASPIRATIONAL DISTRICTS PROGRAMME AS THE REPOSITORY OF IMPLEMENTABLE SOCIAL SECTOR PRACTICES

The Aspirational Districts Programme was formed to comprehensively address development needs and transform 115 districts across 28 states that require the most progress on various development parameters. These districts account for more than 20 per cent of India's population and cover over 8,600 gram panchayats. The programme's emphasis is on improving districts on 49 indicators across five core spheres—education, health and nutrition, financial inclusion, agriculture, skill development and basic infrastructure. The programme is based on real-time data and constant monitoring, and is a collaborative project between the central and state governments in partnership with various philanthropic foundations and the larger civil society. The main attempt is to prioritize resources, concentrate efforts, address governance and capacity bottlenecks in order to accelerate the pace of change in the human development indicators to promote a more fair, equitable and inclusive growth in the country. This is an excellent example of cooperative federalism where various levels of government work together to enhance development in India.

## INDIA'S RAPID ASCENSION TO THE TOP

India's rapid ascension to the top is backed by incredible work done from the grass roots up. And, while challenges remain, the progress visible so far is merely the tip of the iceberg. High-quality jobs will also be created through these initiatives, with the health sector alone expected to generate over 1.5 million jobs in the public sector by 2022. But the biggest impact will be on overall improvement in the human development index of India.

Access to health, education and personal rights to quality of life are becoming barrier-free and attainable. A healthy, educated and motivated next generation is the key that unlocks India's insurmountable potential. Yes, there is work that remains to be done, but just look at how far India has come. By 2030, I anticipate India would have become highly advanced in social sector fulfillment. For India, it is imperative that the momentum on structural reforms in the social sector is accelerated. This alone can ensure a high growth of 9–10 per cent for the next 30 years or more. Consolidating and expanding the work that has already been done will surely get us there.

# Transforming Sanitation: Twin Pits and Toilet Sabhas*

On the nippy morning of Monday, 19 November, we set out before the crack of dawn from Delhi on a road journey to Wajidpur village in Firozabad, Uttar Pradesh. On the occasion of World Toilet Day, we decided to empty a rural toilet pit which had been closed for about a year. This was to demonstrate the safety and efficacy of the twin-pit toilet model, in which decomposed faecal material is transformed into safe-to-use organic manure. We also participated in a unique 'Toilet Sansad', organized by the residents of the village—a first-of-its-kind toilet parliament, a platform for the residents to discuss their issues related to sanitation and reach consensus for collective action.

Prior to 'digging in', we met the family whose toilet pit we were about to empty, and we could sense their curiosity to see what was inside the pit after it had been shut for so long. They were also bemused to see senior civil servants from Delhi drive all the way from Delhi to their village and be interested in emptying their toilet pit. They still welcomed

*Amitabh Kant with Parameswaran Iyer

us warmly, so we took our shovels and proceeded to empty the pit to demonstrate that each household could do so, without depending on external help.

A standard twin-pit toilet model fills up in roughly five years for a six-member family. The waste is then easily redirected to the second pit, and the closed pit's waste becomes safe-to-handle organic compost in about a year's time, rich in nutrients, making it ideal for use in agriculture. In many parts of India, this is also known as sona khaad (golden fertilizer). These last few years, prominent personalities such as the comptroller and auditor general of India, popular Bollywood celebrity, Akshay Kumar, and many district collectors have entered and emptied toilet pits themselves to dispel the myths, biases and stigma associated with pit-emptying and change people's attitudes and behaviours towards toilets. This intense focus on behaviour change is one of the critical initiatives that have made SBM the success it has become.

About a century ago, the Father of the Nation, Mohandas Karamchand Gandhi, shared his vision for a clean India. In a 1927 edition of *Navajivan* magazine, he wrote, 'An ideal village will be so constructed as to lend itself to perfect sanitation... The very first problem the village worker will solve is its sanitation.' But India made very slow progress towards advancing safe sanitation for decades after independence. So how did India—the biggest contributor to open defecation in the world—become the world's largest eliminator of open defecation?

The start was made on Independence Day, 2014, when Prime Minister Narendra Modi, challenged the nation to achieve universal sanitation in five years, thereby putting sanitation at the forefront of his development agenda. In these past four years, the Prime Minister has also put his political capital behind the SBM, truly making it everyone's business. The challenge was immense—we are talking about a country of 1.3 billion people, of which 600 million people were practising open defecation until 2014. Today, that number has reduced to less than 100 million.

There were four main challenges for the SBM, which subsequently became the SBM's biggest opportunities:

- **Scale**: Few programmes across the world have attempted to mainstream sanitation in a country of well over a billion people, with different cultures, beliefs, languages and customs.
- **Speed**: Previous sanitation programmes had not infused a sense of urgency for improvements in sanitation. Consequently, sanitation and toilets were not a priority, and progress was incremental.
- **Sustainability:** Previous programmes had not succeeded in sustaining their achievements. The lack of continuous behaviour change communication, monitoring and evaluation, and institutional arrangements to sustain usage of toilets led to many of them becoming defunct.
- **Stigma**: The earlier programmes only peripherally tackled the core issue of behaviour change, to break the stigma associated with talking about toilets, having a toilet in one's home, cleaning one's toilet, emptying a filled pit and breaking age-old traditions of defecating in the open.

The visit to the village was an extremely enriching experience for us. We particularly appreciated the efforts of the village to democratize the entire process of achieving and sustaining universal sanitation. We were impressed to see the participation of people—women, men, children—of the village in the 'Toilet Sansad'. The setting resembled our parliament where elected representatives debate. The 'Toilet Sansad', after detailed deliberation, made the six swachhata resolutions—levy a fine on any open defecators, convert all single-pit toilets to twin-pit toilets, make a soak pit for any septic tanks, promote composting for organic waste management, use organic fertilizers as far as possible, and eliminate plastic usage.

After a discussion on each resolution, all six were unanimously adopted by the 'Toilet Sabha'. The last resolution was especially interesting as the government of Uttar Pradesh had recently taken a policy decision to ban the use of plastic in the state. This would not be possible unless the state's 100,000 villages stopped using plastic and polythene. Here we were witnessing the resolve of Wajidpur village to implement on the ground the policy decision of the state government. The 'Toilet Sansad' resolved in unison that they would shun the use of plastics.

On our return to Delhi, we discussed how this concept of 'sansad' at local level could be a powerful platform for village transformation. This culture of frank discussion, achieving consensus through consultation and coming together for collective action needs to be scaled up. The key building blocks for this were laid by the collector, Neha Sharma, and her team—creating enabling provisions, awareness, mass mobilization, effective information, education and communication, apart from many other things.

With India's sanitation coverage already over 99.99 per cent, India is truly witnessing a sanitation revolution. We are well and truly on track to become an open defecation free (ODF) nation within the prescribed timelines. Our visit to Wajidpur made us truly believe that the culture on the ground has tremendously changed to one which would make all of us extremely proud.

# Transforming Higher Education

India's greatest asset is its human potential. With over one-sixth of the world's population, and poised to be the youngest country, India stands at an opportune juncture for transformative economic and social progress. Education is, however, a critical element that must be strengthened to attain this potential.

Higher education saw unprecedented action recently in the form of regulatory reforms that address critical challenges.

## LONG-LASTING CHALLENGES

India has one of the world's largest higher-education systems, with over 900 universities, 39,000 colleges, and 3.7 crore students. While the sector's size has grown exponentially over the past seven decades, the regulatory framework has stood almost still in time. The UGC, established under the UGC Act, 1956, in a scenario of 25 universities, has continued to regulate over 900 universities with the same stick.

Long-standing regulations have been criticized for their overly prescriptive and restrictive nature, emphasis on inputs, 'inspector raj' that lacks transparency and objectivity, and continuance of obsolete elements. In many ways, such regulation has fettered dynamism and innovation for enhancing educational quality and relevance.

Another key challenge has been weak-quality assessment or accreditation of existing institutions. The National Assessment and Accreditation Council (NAAC) is the only body recognized to accredit universities and colleges. At best, it can accredit roughly 1000 institutions per year—that is highly impractical for a country with over 41,000 institutions, which further need reaccreditation every five years. No wonder then that roughly 65 per cent universities and 86 per cent colleges lie unaccredited. These inadequacies have created a quality crisis.

## KEY REGULATORY REFORMS

The stagnation and quality crisis brewing in higher education needed to be urgently addressed, and recently, critical reforms were identified and executed.

### *Unfettering Through Graded Autonomy*

New UGC [Categorization of Universities (Only) for Grant of Graded Autonomy] Regulations, 2018, enable greater academic, administrative and financial autonomy for institutions of high quality. Over 60 universities were declared autonomous last year. Universities above specified quality benchmarks (Categories I and II) now have the freedom to start new departments, programmes and courses (including NSQF-consistent skill courses), without requiring UGC approval, in a self-financed mode.

A transparent, merit-based incentive structure can now be created for the faculty, in addition to their existing government pay scales. Institutions can additionally recruit international faculty from the world's top institutions, and admit meritorious international students at fees decided by the institution. Category-I institutions are now exempted from certain inspections. They can also engage in academic collaborations with globally acclaimed universities, open research parks and incubation centres without requiring UGC approval. Regulation shall continue for institutions with lower accreditation scores, where closer checks may be needed to safeguard students' interests and mitigate the risk of fake operations.

The graded autonomy framework can energize the entire system—not only will high-performing institutions be incentivized with greater autonomy, but relatively low-performing institutions shall also be stirred up to try moving up the ladder.

### *Strengthening Quality Assessment*

To nudge institutions towards accreditation, prominent display of accreditation grade or unaccredited status on all public-information material has been made mandatory for institutions. New UGC regulations enable empanelment of additional accreditation agencies. Ongoing reforms are targeted at breaking the existing monopoly of a single-accreditation body. The coverage, credibility and reliability of accreditation is expected to leap ahead with the ongoing reforms.

Additional measures target research quality—screening the quality of journals used to evaluate faculty publications, aptitude-based tests for PhD admissions, and anti-plagiarism measures.

### *Online Degrees for Quality Beyond Barriers*

India's Gross Enrolment Ratio is 25.8 per cent, roughly half of Brazil's or China's. Despite efforts to create new institutions, our demand may not be met by regular, physical institutions alone. To tackle these constraints and expand access to high-quality education, fully online degree programs have been recognized for the first time. UGC (Online Courses or Programmes) Regulations, 2018, enable these to be run by high-grade institutions only, to ensure quality and protect student interests.

### *Unleashing World-class Higher Education*

To simultaneously address the needs of our islands of excellence, which need a thrust to become the global best, a special initiative to develop 'Institutions of Eminence' (IoEs) was launched. IoEs will operate under a special regulatory architecture, with outcome focus, academic freedom and flexibility, high administrative and financial autonomy. Government institutions will be additionally funded. Three government and three private institutions were competitively selected by a committee of eminent national and international experts. Institutions will be regularly reviewed against committed timelines to ensure accountability.

These reforms are unprecedented, not only in how they address long-standing challenges in higher education but also in speed of implementation. In less than three years, regulatory changes not seen for decades have been executed. Work is also in progress on longer-term reforms to drive the legislative framework towards high quality, greater efficiency and transparency, accountability, streamlining of multiple regulators, etc.

# India Needs Doctors: The Need to Disrupt the Medical Education System

India bears a significantly higher burden of diseases in the world. There are vast inequalities in the health status and availability of healthcare resources across the states of India. As per the World Health Organisation (WHO) report (2018), India ranks 67th in the list of 133 developing countries with a doctor-population ratio of 0.50:1000 as compared to a world average of 1.72:1000. In Bihar, one government doctor serves 28,391 people while in Uttar Pradesh there are 19,962 patients per doctor. There are 22 times more engineers than doctors in India. We are finding it impossible to get doctors in Aspirational Districts. This severe shortage of doctors has led to a widespread problem of quackery. Self-styled doctors without formal training provide up to 75 per cent of primary care visits. The WHO reports that 31.4 per cent of those calling themselves allopathic doctors were educated only up to Class XII and 57.3 per cent doctors do not have medical qualifications. A recent study by Centre for Disease Dynamics, Economics and Policy has highlighted that India has a shortage of 600,000 doctors and two million nurses.

Medical education is at the core of availability of quality

healthcare services and provides answers to the healthcare problems in India. However, the availability of medical graduates in India is a severe constraint. With the population increasing annually at the rate of 1.2 per cent, the current annual addition of approximately 70,000 medical doctors into the system is totally insufficient to comply with the WHO benchmark of 1 doctor for every 1,000 people. The problem is further aggravated with a skewed availability of postgraduate seats as compared to undergraduate seats.

An extremely serious concern is the uneven distribution of doctors and imbalanced growth of medical colleges, which is skewed towards urban areas and certain states in the country. Presently, 315 medical colleges are spread over just 188 of the country's 642 districts, and 43 per cent of them are concentrated in five southern states. This is essentially due to the absence of regulation to address the regional disparities in setting up new medical colleges. This situation calls for urgent structural changes to bridge the gap of doctor-to-people ratio in the country without compromising on the quality of medical education.

The MCI, as a regulator, promotes and maintains the quality of allopathic medical education in the country. Unfortunately, over the years, various bottlenecks have been allowed to creep into the system with serious detrimental effects on medical education which have adversely impacted delivery of quality health services. The National Medical Commission (NMC) Bill, based on the recommendations of the Dr Panagariya Committee, had addressed the issue of acute shortage of medical personnel by a series of pathbreaking recommendations. Unfortunately, the bill is still pending.

The Board of Governors, recently constituted in lieu of MCI, need to take it as a challenge and initiate structural reforms. Considering the long gestation period of medical education, even if the reforms are undertaken in the current academic year, they will start having an impact only post 2025. Therefore, the disruption in medical education is so urgent that it cannot be deferred any longer.

## HOW DO WE BRING IN A RADICAL TRANSFORMATION?

First, we need to relook at the compliance requirements for establishing and operating medical colleges in the country. Comparison with international benchmarks reveals that stipulations such as maximum number of medical seats allowed per medical college, OPD (outpatient department) and IPD (inpatient department) requirements and faculty norms are way too rigorous in India. While this prevents genuinely functioning hospitals from venturing into medical education, it allows the suboptimal set-ups to thrive.

Second, we need to rationalize the MCI norms for undergraduate as well as postgraduate education. There is a sharp asymmetry between undergraduate and postgraduate medical seats, with postgraduate seats at less than one-third of the undergraduate seats.

Third, we need to rationalize the faculty-student ratio which in India is almost seven times that of international norms.

Fourth, we need to liberalize the faculty's eligibility requirements. This will allow tapping into the huge pool of qualified non-teaching practitioners available in both public and private health sectors beyond the medical colleges. Norms need to be optimized to allow doctors who are interested in teaching to become part-time or adjunct faculty. In addition, information technology should be leveraged to introduce technology-simulation, telemedicine and use of AI.

Fifth, the capital cost of setting up new medical colleges is almost as high as ₹5 crore per bed. This is mostly because of extensive land and infrastructure requirements. The existing minimum standard requirements mandated by MCI are irrational and they have proved to be the biggest impediment in the establishment and expansion of medical colleges. These rigid requirements have prevented district hospitals, large public sector hospitals (like railways hospitals, army hospitals, ESI, etc.) and large private sector hospitals from becoming teaching hospitals. The existing norms for infrastructure need to be rationalized to give impetus to opening of new medical colleges based on existing infrastructure. This will allow maximization of available resources in both public- and private-sector hospitals without additional huge investments and to fill up the massive shortage of doctors.

Sixth, with the launch of Ayushman Bharat, the healthcare sector in India is expected to enhance its footprints. The road ahead requires that the private and the public sector complement each other in the availability of infrastructure, faculty and a fully functional hospital. The PPP model for the tie-up of private medical colleges with public hospitals will enable the enhancement of the level of services in these hospitals and also facilitate utilization of the already existing clinical material. It will also considerably reduce financial burdens on the government and can contribute towards the normative provision of two beds per 1,000 population.

Even with full political and administrative commitment,

these initiatives will take time and have a gestation period. Alternative measures are required on priority to address the severe imbalance at the primary healthcare level in rural areas.

To my mind, these are:

First, we need to undertake interventions such as reskilling of human resources available in the health sector. For instance, nurses in the UK, Thailand and African countries are increasingly taking on doctors' roles at primary level. Second, there have been commendable examples within the country, such as Chhattisgarh's three-year community medicine course, whose efficacy was validated by studies from Harvard. Third, India needs to develop bridge courses for dental and AYUSH (Ayurveda, Yoga & Naturopathy, Unani, Siddha, Sowa Rigpa and Homeopathy) doctors to allow them to practise after completing the bridge course as community doctors. Fourth, India needs to allow dental doctors who do the three-year common syllabus with doctors to also practise family medicine. Fifth, we need a relaxation in reciprocity so that Indian doctors in the USA, Europe and Australia can come to India and teach.

The aforementioned measures are required to heal the deplorable and continuously deteriorating health situation in the country, particularly in rural areas and at the primary-healthcare level. These initiatives shall go a long way in augmenting the supply side for the critical human resources in the health sector. This alone will increase the accessibility and affordability of the healthcare at a low-opportunity cost.

# The Challenge of Malnutrition and Undernourishment

The recently published NFHS-4 data reveals that India is confronted with severe challenges of an inter-generational cycle of undernutrition. The fact that every second women in India is anaemic, every third child stunted and underweight, and only every second child exclusively breastfed for the first six months of life, is a matter of serious concern, calling for urgent action.

The chronic impact of stunting on lifelong learning and adult productivity, in addition to increased disease susceptibility, is already well-known. Going by the NFHS-4 results, it appears that 40 per cent of our future workforce will be unable to achieve their full physical and cognitive potential. At this pace, unless nutrition is brought at the centre stage, India will miss out on the window of opportunity by failing to capitalize on its demographic dividend.

Although wide disparities exist across states and districts, an analysis of NFHS-4 data shows that the burden of malnourishment is more pronounced in certain areas. For example, out of the 201 districts with the highest percentage of stunted children below five years of age, 53 districts are in Uttar

Pradesh, 36 in Bihar, 27 in Madhya Pradesh, 17 in Jharkhand and 11 in Rajasthan. This shows that if concerted efforts are made in these states, the potential gains can be very high.

So what does India need to do to quickly make a radical transformation in malnutrition and undernourishment? Despite being a complex problem of a multidimensional nature, there are three levers to address the challenge of malnourishment—nutritious food; essential water, sanitation and hygiene (WASH) practices; and behavioural change.

The presence of schemes, such as the National Health Mission (NHM), Integrated Child Development Mission (ICDS), SBM and National Rural Drinking Water Mission clearly shows that funding is not the key constraint. In addition, the recently launched PMMVY (Maternity Benefit Scheme) which will directly transfer cash to pregnant women and lactating mothers upon fulfilment of certain conditions promoting uptake of health services and behavioural change, will complement the existent efforts.

First, to see the desired results, these programmes need to be converged and integrated and effectively implemented at the district level. Although the nutrition agenda has been put centre stage at the central level, it is important that it is made the topmost priority at field levels. Implementation must be followed up through the creation of a nutrition MIS (management information system) which is a comprehensive, Aadhaar-linked, digitized database of every child and of all nutrition indicators. There is a need to track and monitor progress at different levels on a real-time basis and identify states/districts/blocks that are lagging behind.

Second, under the recently revised norms of the current ICDS scheme, pregnant mothers and the newborn child are entitled to receive 'Take Home Ration' worth ₹10,332 over a 45-month period. Unfortunately, this scheme has been plagued in the states with complaints of leakages and poor-quality food supplement. Recently, several pilots have demonstrated the efficacy of implementing conditional cash transfer in the mother's account. This, however, must be accompanied by several enabling conditions.

Third, we must learn from innovative service-delivery models of states like Madhya Pradesh (Suposhan and Sneha Shivirs), Odisha (Ami Bhi Paribu), Chhattisgarh (Nava Jatan) and Maharashtra which use growth monitoring and promotion as the trigger for ensuring universal coverage of services while enabling early preventative action.

Fourth, it is seen that despite the rise in institutional birth rates to almost 80 per cent, early initiation of breastfeeding (within one hour of birth) remains as low as 41.6 per cent. There is an imminent need to promote exclusive breastfeeding for the first six months of life. This calls for skilled counselling, support at field level, extension and mass communication. It is estimated that universalization of optimal breastfeeding practices could reduce around 156,000 child deaths every year in India, mainly by protecting against diarrhoea and pneumonia. Similarly, deficiencies of key vitamins and minerals—vitamin A, iron, iodine and zinc—which continue to co-exist and interact with protein and energy deficits need to be addressed through a multipronged approach.

As per WHO estimates, 50 per cent of malnutrition is associated with repeated diarrhoea or intestinal worm infections due to unhygienic practices, inadequate sanitation and unsafe water. This reduces the capacity of the body to absorb essential nutrients required for growth and development in the early years of life. This lack of WASH costs lives. Various estimates have suggested that the lack of adequate sanitation and hand-washing are responsible for over a lakh child deaths every year in India. For a long time, India had the dubious distinction of contributing to almost 60 per cent of the world's open defecation, in spite of the fact that there have been sanitation programmes in the country for over 30 years now. It took the resolve of the Prime Minster to realize that this is not a problem that can be solved incrementally; rather, it needed a mission-mode approach.

In the past five years, the SBM has gained mass momentum. While the sanitation coverage in rural India stood at a meagre 39 per cent in 2014, in the last few years, it has astronomically grown to almost 70 per cent. More than 25 crore Indians have shunned the practice of open defecation with over 2.5 lakh villages and about 217 districts have become ODF. This change has come due to focus on promoting behaviour change through community approaches. Promising results on the ground have started surfacing.

UNICEF measured the economic impact of SBM on rural households. They carried out a survey in 12 states and estimated that in an ODF village, each family over a 10-year period on an average will save over ₹50,000 per year on account of avoided medical costs, time savings and lives saved. Additionally, there is a one-time increase in the value of their property too. They estimated that the financial savings exceed the financial costs to the household by 4.17 times. Similarly, the Bill and Melinda Gates Foundation have measured the impact of an ODF environment on disease prevalence and nutritional indicators. Their survey in five states, comparing ODF and non-ODF villages, found that on an average, the number of children with diarrhoea in a non-ODF village was 46 per cent more than in an ODF village. The number of children with worms in their stool in a non-ODF village was 78 per cent more than in an ODF village. Seventeen per cent more children were found to be stunted and 58 per cent more children were found to be wasted in the non-ODF villages than in the ODF villages.

The SBM approach is by far the biggest behaviour change programme in the world, and most definitely, the fastest acceleration towards complete sanitation by any country. This will make a far-reaching impact on malnutrition and undernourishment.

Nutrition is India's biggest governance challenge. It requires a multi-sectoral approach, locally appropriate strategies and a people's movement with social mobilization at the grass-roots level. Innovative models with visible results are already being implemented on the ground. Similarly, focused programmes such as the SBM and the PMMVY (Maternity Benefit Scheme) and enhanced spending on mother and children in ICDS clearly reflects the agenda of the government to create a malnourishment-free India. Convergence, nutrition MIS with real-time outcome monitoring of every pregnant women and child, and behavioural change towards hygiene and sanitation hold the key to creating a well-nourished India.

# The Challenge of Water: India's Ability to Manage and Govern Water Will Determine Its Future

The Prime Minister has outlined his vision of ensuring access to piped drinking water through 'Nal Se Jal' to every Indian household by 2024. A new Jal Shakti Ministry has been created to undertake this ambitious task.

Water will determine India's ability to achieve high economic growth, ensure environmental sustainability and improve the quality of life for citizens. India is home to 17 per cent of the world's population but has only 4 per cent of the world's freshwater resources. At present, 75 per cent of Indian households do not have access to drinking water and close to 90 per cent of rural households have no access to piped water. At 1,544 cubic metre per capita annual availability, India is already a water-stressed country and we are advancing towards becoming water-scarce. India today is also the world's largest groundwater extractor, pumping out up to nearly 25 per cent of the global groundwater usage annually. Five of the world's twenty largest cities under water stress are in India, with Delhi being second in the list. Over

20 million wells pump water with the free power supply provided by state governments. Rice and sugar cane, which are both water-guzzling crops, have expanded in water-scarce states, consuming vast amount of irrigation water per hectare. Punjab is using three times more water to produce 1 kg of rice as compared to Bihar and more than twice the water as compared to West Bengal. Almost 80 per cent of the water used for irrigating paddy fields in Punjab is groundwater. India is today exporting more than 10 trillion litres of virtual water through the export of Basmati rice. The recent situation of Chennai running out of freshwater adds further weightage to just how much of a concern water is today.

What does India need to do to meet its biggest challenge—the challenge of water?

First, we need to restore, conserve and augment all our existing local waterbodies. Every panchayat has waterbodies—rivers, ponds, lakes, tanks and wells. Restoring surfaced waterbodies can unlock huge additional water to meet the local requirement. Telangana's Mission Kakatiya is an example, where state waterbodies restoration has led to the restoration of 46,000 water tanks in the state. This initiative has increased water-storage capacity and helped enhance on-farm moisture retention capacity. The Vayalagam Tankfed Agricultural Development Programme by Dhan Foundation has played a key role in restoring and facilitating proper maintenance of tanks in south Indian states. These examples need to be replicated across states.

Second, we need to utilize advanced technology in the management of water. Remote Sensing and Geographic Information System (GIS) can enable real-time data on water and catalyze community to conserve water resources. Every single water asset, including borewells, can be geo-tagged, and the monitoring of groundwater levels can be done on an online platform. Andhra Pradesh has used technology to manage its resources, leading to rise in groundwater levels. States also need to segregate agricultural power-feeders so that electricity consumption, particularly its usage for water extraction, can be measured and monitored. Gujarat has 100 per cent feeder segregation, leading to a major reduction in electricity consumption and effective water management.

Third, community management of water and formation of water users association can lead to success at grass-roots level. A great example of this is in the drought-prone village of Hiware Bazar in Maharashtra. The community initiated watershed management, banned digging of deep borewells and does water budgeting. The village has moved away from water-intensive crops like cotton and sugar cane. This village has inspired and motivated Maharashtra to introduce water budgeting in over 5000 water-stressed villages.

Fourthly, India needs to radically improve its on-farm water efficiency, which is presently amongst the lowest in the world. Our farmers use 3–5 more rounds of water than Chinese, Israeli and American farmers for producing the same amount of crop. There is a disproportionately higher use of water per crop. India utilizes 11.8 $m^3$ per kg of crop produced as compared to 2.28 in China, 4.74 in Israel and 4.78 in the USA. Our farmers need to adopt cropping patterns based on agro-climatic zoning. This would segregate geographic areas based on climate, terrain and hydrological conditions, and farmers will ensure that water is utilized in an optimum manner. The drought-prone region of Bundelkhand, Mentha, which requires 18–22 rounds of irrigation, is cultivated despite water shortage. We need to educate our farmers and modify subsidies and minimum support price (MSP) to disincentivize farmers from growing water-intensive crops. Procuring and providing MSP for millets (jwar, bajra and ragi) and pulses (urad, arhar, chana and moong) will enable better nutrition through mid-day meals and ICDS schemes, and facilitate a shift towards low water consumption and high-protein crops.

Fifth, one of the major catalysts for India's groundwater crisis is the existing legal framework that ties up water rights with land rights and allows landowners to extract unlimited groundwater in an unchecked manner. Groundwater is a finite resource and its excessive withdrawal has severe implications on distribution, sustainability and community. A great example is Maharashtra, which through legislation, has controlled the extraction of groundwater. The Maharashtra Groundwater Development and Management Rules mandate registration and prohibition of wells. Permission for digging new wells necessitates building a groundwater recharge structure alongside. Other states need to learn from this experience.

Sixth, there is an imperative need for a rational and pragmatic policy for pricing water that is supplied to the users. There is huge willingness to pay for the supply of water on a regular basis but huge political and administrative unwillingness to charge for water. This must change. Pricing of water will ensure adequate investment in water infrastructure.

Seventh, for urban areas in India, Singapore is a great example of reducing dependence of water from the neighbouring country, Malaysia, and ensuring universal, affordable, efficient and high-quality water through reuse of waste water, building rainwater catchments, dual piping, desalination as well as water legislation, dynamic water pricing, public education and research and development in water.

Fortunately, there are several good things happening on ground. States have taken the initiative to implement schemes aimed at water conservation and artificial recharge. Jalyukt Shivar in Maharashtra, Mukhya Mantri Jal Swavalamban Abhiyan in Rajasthan, Mission Kakatiya in Telangana, and Sujalam Sufalam in Gujarat have brought water centre stage and are making a difference on ground. In Maharashtra, under Jalyukt Shivar, nearly 11,000 villages were made drought-free by creating water harvesting structures. It also resulted in a groundwater table rise by 1.5 to 2 m. Jabalpur, Indore and Gwalior municipal corporations have granted rebate on property tax for rainwater harvesting facility. In Telangana, nearly 17,000 minor irrigation tanks were restored which helped in supply of collected rainwater to 19 lakh acres of agricultural land. NITI Aayog has developed the composite water management index (CWMI) which ranks states on the management of water and explains states progress in 28 indicators relating to water management.

We need a water-secure India. Our ability to manage and govern our water resources efficiently will determine our ability to grow and prosper.

# Aspirational Districts: Transforming India, One District at a Time

It is a well-known fact that India is on a high-growth trajectory. What was urgently needed however was the enhancement of the human development index and the reduction in the significant inter-state and inter-district variations in development. For this to happen, the Prime Minister felt that the aspirational districts had to be transformed, and launched the 'Transformation of Aspirational Districts' programme in January 2018.

The programme hinges on expeditiously transforming 115 districts that were identified from 28 states, in a transparent manner. There are three core aspects that frame the structure of the programme—convergence (of central and state schemes), collaboration (of central, state-level 'prabhari' officers and district collectors), and competition among districts. Driven primarily by the states and instituted for the states, this initiative focuses on the strength of each district, and identifies the attainable outcomes for immediate improvement, while measuring progress and ranking the selected districts.

Operationally, the officers at the level of additional secretary have been nominated to become the 'central prabhari officers' of each district, while states have appointed state-nodal and prabhari officers. An empowered committee under my convenorship has been instituted to help in the convergence of various government schemes and streamlining of efforts. The districts were considered after consultation with state officials using a composite index of key data sets. The prabhari officers provide feedback and recommendations based on their findings, and the empowered committee then makes necessary amendments on an ongoing basis based on the feedback. This ensures the effective utilization of flexi funds for districts under the programme.

To optimally utilize potential and ensure that the New India 2022 is a part of every individual's vision, especially in the rural areas, this initiative focuses closely on improving people's ability to participate fully in the rapidly growing economy. After several rounds of consultations, it was decided that the baseline ranking for the 115 aspirational districts would be based on 49 indicators across five sectors that includes health and nutrition (30 per cent) through 13 indicators, education (30 per cent) through 8 indicators, agriculture and water resources (20 per cent) through 10 indicators, financial inclusion and skill development (10 per cent) through 10 indicators, and basic infrastructure (10 per cent) through 7 indicators.

The districts were selected through a transparent process, keeping the capacity of states in mind. Fifty districts were allocated across 12 ministries. Thirty-five districts that were in the LWE areas were allocated to the Ministry of Home Affairs, and 30 districts have been allocated to NITI Aayog.

There will be an annual ranking of the performance of districts. Objective and measurable indicators have been identified in focus sectors. These are going to be benchmarked with the best performing districts in India. Since the progress will be captured on a real-time basis, a dashboard has been formulated that features a real-time monitoring mechanism. The key tangible outcomes will be as follows:

a) What is measured is expected to improve rapidly across states
b) A cooperative competition among districts is a vital strategy
c) Eventually, this initiative is expected to help fine-tune government programmes

As of 1 April 2018, districts have started entering data. To help evaluate progress and the success of initiatives introduced by the central government in collaboration with the states, a delta ranking of these districts will be displayed every month from May 2018 on the dashboard based on the 'incremental progress' to be monitored on a real-time basis. To ensure transparency in real-time, the dashboard will be open to the public to monitor the progress of the aspirational districts. Among other outcomes, senior officials have felt the initiative will highlight the importance of convergence of the efforts of Accredited Social Health Activists (ASHA), Auxiliary Nurse Midwives (ANMs) and Anganwadi workers, and the social capital can make a remarkable difference, given the fact that 8,603 gram panchayats are covered in the aspirational districts.

This programme is non-partisan and completely unbiased. It is an all-India initiative meant to trigger uniform growth and development in every corner of the country. Simply put, it is a landmark unprecedented achievement for e-monitoring, governance and productive use of real-time data through a participatory method that involves everyone. Something like this has never been attempted before, let alone achieved, and this is the first step in ensuring a national inclusive development strategy that is broad-based and ensures that no district is left behind.

Don't mistake this to merely be a name-and-shame module—this is far more than that. This is essentially a competitive federalism and synergy-enhancing module that will eventually give every corner of India—rural or urban—a chance to exceed its own aspirations, and a platform to be heard, and where required, helped. The initiative is supported by prestigious partners in programme implementation which provide ground-level support, like the Tata Trust, Piramal Foundation, ITC and L&T, as well as the Bill & Melinda Gates Foundation and IDInsight to conduct surveys. The partners will ably support the programme through leadership development, change management, technology integration and by implementing various innovative practices.

NITI Aayog and all associated ministries are working closely with the states towards a transparent, inclusive and accountable India. With a dedicated team committed to this project, this is an immersive initiative that will change the landscape of how India progresses through the vision of the Government of India.

Our focus is to improve India in the Human Development Index ranking, raising the living standards of its citizens and ensuring inclusive growth for all. Unless these districts are brought up to the parameters that each of us expects from our own lives, India will not be able to progress at the rapid pace that would otherwise be achieved from the government's broad range of initiatives and development strategy. With the help of this initiative, much will be achieved towards uniform development. It is unquestionable that the 'Transformation of Aspirational Districts' initiative, envisioned by the Hon'ble Prime Minister, is a giant leap towards transforming India for the New India 2022 vision—one district at a time.

# Nudging India to Progress: Performance in Health Outcomes Index

The release of 'Healthy States, Progressive India' report has spurred a vibrant debate on the status and future of India's health sector. Understandably, the focus has been on the 'Performance in Health Outcomes', a reaction of the performance, and annual progress of states and UTs on myriad health indicators. India is committed to the UN Sustainable Development Goals (SDGs) to ensure 'good health and well-being' of all its citizens. This index will help nudge states towards improving their health sector outcomes in the spirit of cooperative and competitive federalism.

Kerala is the leader among large states, closely followed by Punjab and Tamil Nadu. Uttar Pradesh, Rajasthan and Bihar are the least performing states. Mizoram is the best performing small state, followed by Manipur, while Nagaland and Tripura take the final two spots. Lakshadweep secured the top spot among UTs, and Dadra and Nagar Haveli is at the end of the rankings. The goal of the index is not just to rank states based on their historical performance, but also on their incremental performance. The attempt is to capture the change made during the course of the year. Jharkhand, Jammu and Kashmir, and Uttar Pradesh are ranked first, second and third, respectively, in the incremental performance ranking. However, the rankings alone don't tell us the whole story.

The 'Performance in Health Outcomes' index is made up of 24 indicators in three different domains—health outcomes, governance and information, and key inputs and processes. While 'health outcomes' accounts for 70 per cent of the weight, it is important not to ignore the other two domains which weigh 12 per cent and 18 per cent, respectively. The 'health outcomes' domain has indicators such as TFR (total fertility rate), NMR (neonatal mortality rate), SRB (sex ratio at birth), etc. The governance and information domain measures the quality of data ('data integrity' indicator) and the average occupancy in important health-related posts such as principal secretary (health), chief medical officer, etc. Key inputs and processes measure the current status of healthcare professional vacancies, infrastructure at district hospitals, and the speed of financial governance in the states.

Kerala topped the overall index with a score of 76.55 in the reference year (2015–16). The state's performance is even more stellar if we consider just the 'health outcomes' domain, where it has improved its performance year-on-year to 82.89, a 13.02-points lead over Punjab. Incremental progress will be tougher as it has already achieved or exceeded several of the goals and targets in the National Health Policy (NHP) and the SDGs. However, a closer look at the indicators reveals major concerns. Sex ratio at birth has fallen to 967, while the proportion of infants with low birth weight has gone up to 11.7 per cent. The proportion of fully immunized children has also gone down in Kerala state. At the same time, it has fallen short in 'key inputs and processes' domain, falling to 69.62 in 2015–16, a 4.55-points drop.

## WHAT ARE THE KEY RESULTS THAT EMERGE FROM THE HEALTH INDEX?

First, there are large gaps between the states. The gap between the best performing states and the least performing states is worrisome. Kerala and Uttar Pradesh are separated by 42.86 points, Mizoram and Nagaland by 36.32, and Lakshadweep and Dadra and Nagar Haveli by 31.15 (see Table 1). Two-thirds of our citizens live in states with an overall score of less than 60.

Second, incremental performance reveals that there has been a decline in performance on some states. While most states have registered an increase in their health index in 2015–16 relative to 2014–15, scores of six states (Kerala, Haryana, Gujarat, Karnataka, Himachal Pradesh, and Uttarakhand) have declined. These states need to progress on health index parameters for continuous improvement.

Third, India has made significant strides in achieving the goals set out under the SDGs and our own NHP. Some of our states have already met or exceeded the goals a decade ahead of 2030 (see Table 2).

**Table 1:**
**Gap between best performing and least performing states**

| Index | Best Performing State | | Least Performing State | | Gap |
|---|---|---|---|---|---|
| Overall Index | Kerala | 76.55 | Uttar Pradesh | 33.69 | 42.86 |
| Health Index | Kerala | 82.89 | Rajasthan | 29.58 | 53.31 |
| Key Inputs and Processes | Tamil Nadu | 78.06 | Uttar Pradesh | 25.02 | 53.04 |

**Table 2:**
**UNSDG & NHP goals and state performances**

| | Health Indicator | UNSDG | NHP | Best Performer | Least Performer |
|---|---|---|---|---|---|
| 1 | Neonatal Mortality Rate | Under 12 by 2030 | Under 16 by 2025 | Kerala (6) | Odisha (35) |
| 2 | Under 5 Mortality Rate | Under 25 by 2030 | Under 23 by 2025 | Kerala (13) | Assam, Madhya Pradesh (62) |
| 3 | Total Fertility Rate | Below replacement level (2.1) | | Tamil Nadu, West Bengal (1.6) | Bihar (3.3) |
| 4 | Low Birth Weight | NA | NA | Telangana (5.7) | Rajasthan (25.5) |
| 5 | Sex Ratio at Birth | NA | NA | Kerala (967) | Haryana (831) |

## WHAT ARE THE LESSONS THAT EMERGE FROM THE HEALTH OUTCOMES INDEX?

First, an exercise of this kind requires data on health outcomes which are periodic, reliable and comparable across different states and UTs. The effort did show us significant gaps in the availability of such data, especially for the smaller states. We need robust programmatic data that can be used for continuous monitoring.

Second, incentives need to be linked to performance. The two separate rankings, on absolute performance and year-on-year progress, are designed to encourage states to work on their health sector and bring about meaningful transformation. The linking of the health index with incentives under National Health Mission will further push states to improve outcomes. NITI Aayog is creating a framework to track the performance of government hospitals based on outcome metrics. Together with the upgrading and setting up of health and wellness centres under the Ayushman Bharat Scheme and the National Health Protection Scheme, these measures will help us realize the goal of 'good health and well-being' for all of India's citizens.

# Transforming India's Healthcare Delivery through Ayushman Bharat Yojana*: Focus on Primary Healthcare and Insurance Are Steps Towards Universal Health Coverage

The sight of a family teetering at the brink of hope and despondency, surviving and falling into economic ruin on account of ill health is distressingly common. That one episode of hospitalized care eats away the entire accumulated assets and sends the family into a spiral of unsustainable debt, chronic sickness and social, economic and psychological trauma that transcends generations. India's government health expenditure at 1.13 per cent of its GDP is the lowest amongst the emerging developing countries. In contrast, China's expenditure is 2.45 per cent and Thailand 2.90 per cent of its GDP. Out-of-pocket expenses, which are catastrophic, push nearly 66 lakh households of India into poverty every year. 24.9 per cent of households in rural areas and 18.2 per cent in urban areas meet medical

*Amitabh Kant and Indu Bhushan

expenditures through borrowings, and 17.3 per cent of India's population spend more than 10 per cent of their household budget in accessing health services. These expenditures are not only heavily debilitating for families but are also highly regressive in their impact. The poorest of the poor are the worst impacted.

The Ayushman Bharat Yojana demonstrates a strong resolve on the part of the government to address this issue by ensuring primary healthcare through the establishment of 150,000 health and wellness centres. These centres provide comprehensive healthcare and are not only responsible for providing essential drugs and diagnostic services and are also digitally linked to the district hospitals. The health and wellness centres also have convergence with yoga and ayurveda. The first health and wellness centre was launched by the Prime Minister in the aspirational district of Bijapur in May 2018 in Chattisgarh. The second key component of Ayushman Bharat Yojana is the Pradhan Mantri Jan Arogya Yojana (PMJAY) that provides ₹5 lakh cover to around 50 crore economically weaker citizens of India and was launched on 23 September 2018. This is the world's largest government-sponsored healthcare scheme covering a population size equal to the population of the US, Canada and Mexico.

The mission provides in-patient care in empanelled network of healthcare providers (secondary and tertiary care) for more than 1,300 packages in specialties ranging from general medical and surgical procedures to cardiovascular and oncological procedures. The benefits are available to all entitled beneficiaries and are purely cashless, paperless, portable, and backed by a world-class IT infrastructure that provides seamless service delivery at all points of care. The mission leverages capacities available in both public and private sector hospitals while providing standardized high-quality care, with strong fraud protection mechanisms and efficient, service-driven architecture that aims to transform the Indian healthcare systems in the years to come.

The National Health Agency (NHA) and the State Health Agencies (SHAs) are the keystones for the strategic purchasing of medical services at such a massive scale. The NHA is the instrumentality to expand coverage, benefits and financial protection—the three axes of universal healthcare. As a substantive purchaser implementing PMJAY, the NHA and the SHAs use the tools of pricing and incentives to drive down costs of services in the healthcare sector. The rates that were fixed for the procedures went through a rigorous vetting mechanism in more than 50 cities in the country.

The PMJAY relies heavily on fraud detection and monitoring and building complex, intelligent systems that trigger and raise red flags on suspicious transactions, built upon extensive diagnostic guidelines and self-learning pattern-recognition algorithms. The aim is to build a world-class intelligent system for fraud mitigation, grievance redressal, monitoring and evaluation, and research that allows the programme to scientifically evolve. Preauthorization protocols were defined for 621 fraud prone and high-cost procedures for ensuring discipline in the provider network.

The states are the key partners in this alliance and the scheme architecture allows the states freedom for innovations and context-specific customizations. The states have been given flexibility to push for providing greater IPD care through public institutions as well as framework for upgrading their infrastructure. The portability of services across a pan-India network provides beneficiaries in the migrant community to access services without hindrances.

The PMJAY is a truly disruptive influence over the healthcare system in India. As this ambitious programme has found its feet, it has presented India an opportunity to move towards a mature, data-driven, intelligent, predictive health systems built on top of individualized, secure and access-controlled health records, a verified provider registry and tech-enabled drugs and diagnostics supply chains. The mission carries the seeds of transforming not just public health delivery but the entire healthcare sector itself in the next few years.

India through health and wellness centres is finally shifting the focus of healthcare provision towards providing primary healthcare to its citizens. The care on prevention and early management of healthcare has reduced the need for complicated specialist care and out-of-pocket expenses. PMJAY, while catering to 50 crore beneficiaries, will leverage facilities in both private and public hospitals. This comprehensive healthcare system, linking primary, secondary and tertiary care, has the potential to transform the health delivery system for the people of India.

FOUR

# INFRASTRUCTURE

# Urbanization as the Key Driver of India's Growth

Recent studies have projected that India will face an unprecedented scale of urbanization—350 million Indians will move to cities by 2030. This number is likely to double to 700 million by 2050. This is 2.5 times the size of the USA's present population and will be the largest urban movement in the world. This implies that every minute during the next 20 years, 30 Indians will leave rural India for settling in urban areas. Management guru, late C.K. Prahalad had emphasized the imperative need for India to create 500 new cities to accommodate and provide a better-quality life to its migrating people. Otherwise every existing city will become a slum when India turns 75 in 2022.

Cities are centres of growth, innovation and creativity. In today's world, it is not countries but cities that compete for resources and investment. The GDPs of New York and Tokyo are at par with India's GDP. Not a single Indian city figures amongst the top 100 cities of the world. Mumbai ranks 114th and Delhi a dismal 214th. The future of India's growth process lies in the dynamism and vibrancy of its cities. In India, farming accounts for more than 58 per cent of its workforce but accounts for only 14.2 per cent of the GDP. Agriculture can sustain a growth rate of 3 per cent while the Indian economy must grow at 9–10 per cent to lift vast segments of its population above the poverty line. No country in the world has grown on a sustained basis for long periods on the back of its agricultural sector. It is, therefore, inevitable that people will migrate from rural India to towns and cities.

India, like China, has been a reluctant urbanizer. India's freedom movement and the Gandhian worldview were rural development-oriented, with the village being a self-sustained economic unit. Similar was the case with China's peasantry-led revolution. In the early 1870s, China realized that its economic growth and employment creation could not be achieved through the agricultural sector. It recognized that urbanization was an essential feature of economic development and a major component of industrialization and modernization.

For China, economic development was, in essence, about shifting people from sustenance farming to manufacturing, and urbanization was the spatial manifestation of this shift. As a policy, it adopted rapid planned urbanization with manufacturing as the key locomotive. The development of new cities and expansion of existing ones has been a dominant feature of China's growth in the last three decades. Starting with the development of a planned city in Suzhou in partnership with Singapore, China has gone ahead to develop a large number of new cities through a successful business model of monetization of land values. In fact, mayors have been competing with each other to create new cities and successful mayors have gone on to rise rapidly in the Communist Party hierarchy.

In sharp contrast, in post-independence India, the only cities we have created are the capital cities of Chandigarh and Gandhinagar. The only major urban scheme India had launched in its entire planning process was the Jawaharlal Nehru Urban Renewal Mission. A recent report has highlighted that, by 2020, India will face a housing shortage of 30 million dwelling units, 200 million water connections will be required, 350 million people will have to be given access to sewage, 160 GW of power-generating capacity will have to be added and the number of vehicles on roads will increase fivefold. There is, therefore, an overriding need to rejuvenate and revitalize India's existing towns and cities and create new Greenfield cities. The cost of not doing anything will be enormous and would seriously retard India's growth process.

The present government has provided a fresh impetus to urbanization by focusing on the 100 Smart Cities Programme. Rejuvenating Indian cities to enhance the quality of life is a critical necessity. By creating quality trunk infrastructure, recycling water and waste, and developing smart grids, we can make a quantum jump. This requires integrated planning, detailed engineering, walk-to-work concepts and embedding our cities with public transportation. Smart cities, too, require smart people. The Indian citizens must become a proud owner and a key stakeholder of this urbanization process.

While India is a late starter, it has significant advantages of being able to use technology to leapfrog stages of development and learn from good practices in other parts of the world. When cities were made in the USA, gas and water were cheaply available. Vertical utilities were created and cities were made for cars and not people. Today, digital technology enables us to create intelligent and smart cities with a central command room, horizontally managing power, water, transportation and public safety. We need to create cities which are compact, dense and vertical, evolve along efficient mass-transit systems, and encourage cycling and walking.

Most of the lessons of sustainable urbanization emerge from Asian countries. A great example is Kitakyushu in Japan which, post-World War II, was the most polluted city of the world and is today a unique example of pollution control, recycling, green technology and clean environment. Singapore is an example of innovative integrated water management approaches, using reclaimed water, recycling and desalination. In 2010, 30 per cent of its supply of water came from reclaimed water, 20 per cent from collected rainfall and 10 per cent from seawater desalination. Water is, therefore, affordable, efficient and of high quality. Yokohama has reduced waste generation by almost 38.7 per cent, leading to a saving of $1.1 billion of capital cost, otherwise required for installing incinerators. Its waste reduction between 2001–07 resulted in a reduction of 8,40,000 tonnes of $CO_2$ emissions.

As India urbanizes, it will face severe challenges. But there are huge opportunities for smart and sustainable growth which can have a dramatic impact on the quality of life of the expected 700 million urban citizens.

# Transforming India Through High-Speed Bullet Trains

Ezra Vogel, whose 1979 classic *Japan as Number One: Lessons for America* became a bestseller, believed that Japan will revitalize itself through technology, transportation and economic integration with Asia. In many ways, the high-speed train collaboration between Japan and India vindicated his belief.

The foundation stone for the Mumbai Ahmedabad High Speed Railway (MAHSR) project, laid on 14 September 2017, by the two prime ministers is a huge leap towards India and Japan, converging and integrating them in a long-term sustainable economic relationship. The project will enable Indians to learn the Japanese art of perfection in engineering and execution along with innovation and sustainable practices through the 'Make in India' initiative. The launch also culminates a long process of preparations and negotiations between the two countries. It is an occasion to reflect back on some of the key aspects of the project and the process that was followed in achieving this milestone.

The first firm step towards implementation of the MAHSR project was the initiation of the detailed feasibility report by the

Japan International Cooperation Agency (JICA) and Ministry of Railways. Work on the feasibility report started in 2013 and concluded in July 2015. However, the formal decision to go ahead with the project was only taken after a rigorous project appraisal was undertaken by the Committee on Innovative Collaborations which was set up in 2015 to consider such high-value projects. This committee comprised vice chairman NITI Aayog, chairman railway board, secretaries of DIPP and the Department of Economic Affairs, former cabinet secretary R.M. Chandrasekhar and ex-central vigilance commissioner Mr P. Shankar. The issues which were considered in detail by this committee included the relevance of high-speed rail for India and why the Japanese proposal was technologically and financially the best. The project could be taken forward as it had a high level of political commitment driven by the prime minister himself who wanted high-speed transportation to reach the masses in India.

The argument for HSR rests on the fact that HSR is a different level of technology and India can ill-afford to ignore this technology at this stage of its national development. A network of HSR in the longer run would facilitate travelling with enhanced passenger comfort, safety and environmental benefits. An HSR system would also release capacity of existing rail lines, freeing them up, and thus, enabling faster movement of freight and passenger traffic on the existing lines. The HSR system also releases capacity of airports as short-haul flights get curtailed. This freed-up capacity in turn could be utilized for longer duration flights that improve the economics of air transport as well. In addition, development of new cities, promotion of manufacturing to supply equipment and components for the HSR system would provide employment to a growing and better-skilled workforce. Investment in HSR is a highly beneficial system because of its various spin-offs, including infusion of new technology in the country which in the long run would lead to improvement in the operations of the existing railway network as well. The project is being structured in a manner that it leads to large-scale manufacturing of rolling stock, signalling systems and other electrical equipment and components under the 'Make in India' initiative.

At present, 15 countries operate HSR systems. Japan was the first country which set up the HSR in 1964. China has been a late entrant to the HSR system (2008) but now accounts for 46 per cent of the total route length of 21,427 km/hour currently in existence. The countries which operate large HSR systems in the world are Japan, China, France, Germany and Spain. As far as the availability of technology to India was concerned, all the major suppliers, i.e. Japan, China and European counties, were willing to share technology with us. However, the crucial factor which convinced the Committee on Innovative Collaborations to decide in favour of Japan was that it was the only country which offered both technology as well as a unique funding package for the HSR project. The Committee also deliberated whether to make investment in HSR or to use the available funds for strengthening the existing Indian Railway network. The concessional funding proposed by the Government of Japan for the HSR project was specific to the HSR project between Mumbai and Ahmedabad and was not available to the Government of India and the Ministry of Railways for strengthening the existing rail network. The project cost of ₹88,000 crore is being funded through a 50-year soft loan at 0.1 per cent interest rate with a 50-year repayment period and 15-year moratorium.

Apart from the availability of funds, the Japanese Shinkansen technology was preferable for a variety of reasons. It is the oldest HSR system. It operates trains at a speed of over 320 km/hour. The Japanese HSR system has the best safety record in the world with no passenger fatalities in the last 50 years. The Chinese system, which is the largest system at present in terms of route, is of recent origin. There have been fatalities on the Chinese system. On-time performance of Japanese Railways is by far the best in the world. The average delay time per trip is within one minute. The Japanese system is disaster-resistant with earthquake detention system kicking in in the event of an earthquake, which halts the train immediately. Japan's offer of technology is accompanied by an extremely comprehensive training programme for Indian Railway engineers and setting up of a high-speed training Institute at Vadodara. Another very important feature of the Japanese collaboration is their offer to transfer technology and 'Make in India,' including the manufacture of rolling stock in India. It will be a world-beating combination if Japanese technology can combine with the large cost-effective engineering skills available in India so that India can become a hub for manufacturing world-class rolling stock which can be exported all over the world as it has happened in the case of the automobile sector.

Now that the foundation stone has been laid, the work is cut out for the engineers of Indian implementing agency, National High-Speed Rail Corporation Limited (NHSRCL) who are being assisted by the consultants from JICA. It is one of the largest Japanese overseas projects. While the earlier opening was scheduled for 2023, now it has been preponed to 2022 to coincide with the 75th year of India's independence. The MAHSR project is 507-km long and connects Bandra Kurla

Complex in Mumbai to Sabarmati/Ahmedabad in Gujarat. It has 12 stations between Mumbai and Sabarmati (Mumbai, Thane, Virar, Boisar, Vapi, Bilimora, Surat, Bharuch, Vadodara, Anand, Ahmedabad and Sabarmati). The maximum design speed is 350 km/hour and the operating speed is planned to be 320 km/hour. The rolling stock will have 10-car trains (750 seats) in the beginning and 16-car trains (1200 seats) in the future. The project envisages running 35 trains per day at the beginning of the project which will go up to 105 trains per day in 2053. Daily users would be approximately 36,000 persons per day (both ways) i.e. 13 million per annum at the beginning of the project which will go up to 186,000 (or 68 million per annum) by 2053. The total journey time of a fast train will be 2.07 hours and the time a train will stop at each station will be 2.58 hours with the average tariff as 1.5 times of First AC fare.

The high-speed project marks a beginning of a new era for inter-city transportation in India. While the executing agencies are involved in executing this technologically challenging project, national planners should apply their minds to develop a roadmap for future HSR projects as well as other aspects, such as the safety certifications for such projects for extending the technology to other parts of the country.

Japanese have demonstrated their excellence in the Delhi Metro. They are partners in the western stretch of the Dedicated Freight Corridor and the Delhi-Mumbai Industrial Corridor Project. These projects, along with high-speed trains, open up a vast array of opportunities. The Japanese realize that India is not merely a potential but a reality. They also comprehend that India's future is in infrastructure, transportation and urbanization. In these fields, the story has just begun in India whereas it is almost over in other markets. India needs next-generation technology to leapfrog. In cutting-edge technology, the Japanese companies are highly advanced—they innovate, they are perfectionists and several companies work together in a consortium. The high-speed train will act as a huge social and psychological change act. It should change the mindset of Indians, particularly the railways, and teach them the art of excellence, safely, punctuality and perfection.

Professor Donald Keene who had taught for more than fifty years at Columbia University announced his decision at the age of 89 to become a Japanese citizen and live his last days in Japan. He said, 'If any civilization has constantly suffered tragedies and always bounced back, it is Japan. It is because they believe in discipline, team work and perfection. I want to live with these people. I want to die with these people.'

It is this uniqueness which Japan brings to India through the high-speed train project. It can catalyze Indian Railways to transform itself and become a global leader in size, scale, skill and safety.

# Ro-Ro Ferry Service and Its Impact on Transportation and Logistics

Prime Minister Narendra Modi's launch of the first of its kind, state-of-the-art Ro-Ro Ghogha-Dahej and subsequently Hazira project (in Phase 2) marks the beginning of a radical transformation of the transportation and logistics sector in India. The logistic costs in India are extremely high and tapping the full potential of waterways will provide a huge impetus to movement of people, goods, commodities and vehicles. Reducing the cost and time will have an immensely beneficial impact on India's manufacturing and exports. For example, the highly challenging infrastructure project of Ro-Ro ferry plying the Gulf of Khambhat between peninsular Saurashtra and south Gujarat will reduce the time of travel from eight hours to a mere one hour and the distance would be reduced to 31 km from the current distance of 360 km.

India has nearly 14,500 km of navigable inland waterways and around 7,517 km of coastline, which on being developed effectively for transportation purpose, shall help decongest roads and rail networks and offer a multiplier effect to the overall economic development of the regions. Coastal shipping and inland water transport are fuel-efficient, environment-friendly and cost-effective modes of transportation, especially for bulk goods. Emissions from container vessels range from 32 to 36 gCO2 per tonne-km, while from heavy-duty road transport vehicles, it ranges from 51-91 gCO2 per tonne-km. At the same time, the road transportation on an average costs ₹1.5 per tonne-km. For railways it is ₹1.0 per tonne-km, and for waterways it is 25 to 30 paisa per tonne-km only. One litre of fuel can move 24 tonne-km cargo through road transport and 85 tonne-km through rail transport, while it can move as much as 105 tonne-km through water transport. These figures strengthen the assertion that waterways offer a much more economical and environment-friendly mode of transportation vis-à-vis surface transportation. The country can save $50 billion per year if logistics costs reduce from 14 per cent to 9 per cent of the GDP. Reduced logistics costs would in return bring down prices of products.

Out of the total stretch of navigable inland waterways in India, nearly 5,200 km (36 per cent) of major rivers and around 485 km (3 per cent) of canals are conducive to the movement of mechanized vessels. Inland waterways provide several advantages over rail and road transportation by virtue of their operational cost-effectiveness (60–80 per cent lower per tonne-km), lower environmental impact, convenient interoperability and fewer issues in relation to land acquisition and infrastructure development. Currently, only 4,500 km of inland waterways is being commercially utilized and waterways carry less than 1 per cent of domestic cargo in India.

The government's objective has been to develop and operate inland waterways transportation by working towards harnessing this tremendous potential under National Waterways

Act 2016. For the holistic development of India's coastline, the government has launched 'Sagarmala' programme in March 2015 and a National Perspective Plan (NPP) for the comprehensive development of India's coastline has been prepared under it.

Roll-on and Roll-off ('Ro-Ro') waterways projects comprise Ro-Ro ships/vessels which are designed to carry wheeled cargo, such as cars, trucks, semi-trailer trucks, trailers and railroad cars that are driven on and off the ship on their wheels or using a platform vehicle. It also comprises jetties, with related port terminal and approach-connectivity infrastructure. While passenger jetties are used solely to ferry passengers, Ro-Ro jetties have built-in or shore-based ramps that allow the cargo to be efficiently rolled on and off the vessel when in port. The Ro-Ro project in Gujarat will be able to carry up to 100 vehicles (cars, buses and trucks) and 250 passengers between the two terminals. Historically, with limited alternatives available, road transport in the region has always been congested and packed. Also, as the Ro-Ro ferry operators have proposed fares which are at par with prevalent bus fares, the facility shall provide the much-needed respite to the passengers in the region.

In India, various Ro-Ro projects in Assam, Gujarat, Karnataka, Maharashtra and Kerala have the potential to fully open up the vast potential of India's interior areas which have been geographically disadvantaged. Linking up with waterways will transform this disadvantage into a massive advantage.

Most of these Ro-Ro projects in India are being implemented either on event-driven process chain mode, with operation and maintenance being undertaken by the state government, or with more recent projects like the one in Maharashtra, on PPP-DBFOT (design, build, finance, operate, transfer) mode with construction, along with operation and maintenance being undertaken by the private concessionaire. In view of the global competition for pricing of goods and the need to bring about social and economic prosperity to regions, it is imperative that the government develops integrated and efficient modes of transportation system comprising several layers, each of which needs to be developed in a vibrant and efficient manner. One such layer of transportation is the waterways.

One of the key attributes of the investment in water-based transportation is that, unlike many land-based transport systems which require complex land acquisition, rights-of-way, resettlement and other issues, the water-based transportation project proposal is a relatively straightforward initiative. It also steers clear of many legal, regulatory, social and environmental issues which normally affect other transport projects. Further, under a PPP-DBFOT model, the concessionaire receives berthing charges from ferry operators, and parking revenue at terminal. A Ro-Ro project in India, due to infrastructure constraints and overall population and economic growth, generates a project IRR in excess of 10 per cent and is thereby financially viable on a stand-alone level. However, these projects have a huge multiplier impact and should therefore be looked at from the perspective of economic and social rate of return. The state governments can, therefore, consider the awarding of new Ro-Ro projects to private parties on the PPP-DBFOT model, while the existing operational projects can be awarded under the PPP-Reverse BOT (build, operate, transfer) model. Under a suitable PPP model, the government retains the ownership and control of critical national infrastructure, while at the same time it reduces the financing burden on the government and improves the operational efficiency of the asset. In Greenfield projects, the terminals need to be constructed by the government so as to make operations commercially feasible for private sector.

Ro-Ro services are also planned to be implemented by Indian Railways on rails too. Indian Railways is launching the Ro-Ro service in Bihar for cargo vehicles and in Tripura for petro product. In all these Ro-Ro projects, the government is simultaneously also planning and preparing itself for the provision of concrete bridge infrastructure in due course as and when the traffic volume justifies the investment.

The World Bank Report 2016 on Logistics Performance Index (LPI) now ranks India at 35th position as against the 54th rank it occupied in the 2015 report published in early 2014. In 2018, India's rank was 44 in the same index. In order to improve on its LPI ranking further, provisions of integrated mobility across different modes are being prioritized. It is also proposed to adopt superior standard engineering consultancy services and a suitable model for project implementation in order to optimally allocate risks and rewards among the stakeholders. With this the government shall be able to increase the efficacy of transport project implementation across the nation. As the Prime Minister said, this will reduce India's dependence on import of diesel and petrol and take India to a new trajectory of growth.

# Electrifying India's Transport: An Action Plan for Leapfrogging Towards a Clean, Connected and Shared Future

India's urban population will nearly double in the next decade. More than half a billion people will live and work in Indian cities. Travel within and between cities will grow exponentially. This rapid growth poses several social, economic and environmental challenges. To convert these challenges into opportunities, India needs to prioritize shared and public modes of transportation and turn to new sunrise industries that can help combat pollution, reduce congestion, strengthen energy security and also create jobs.

Recently, the union government approved the second phase of the Faster Adoption and Manufacturing of Electric Vehicles scheme (FAME-II) and the National Mission on Transformative Mobility and Battery Storage. Both these actions signal India's commitment to transforming its mobility system. The focus on electrification as the primary technology pathway to achieve this transformation presents India with a powerful opportunity to emerge as a leader in clean, connected and shared mobility solutions, battery manufacturing and renewable energy integration.

The cost of the key components for electric vehicles (EVs), most notably, lithium-ion batteries, have been falling at rates comparable to declines for LED lamps, solar panels and integrated circuit chips. Rapid scaling of the manufacturing of these components in India will further drive down costs, making EVs the most cost-efficient solutions for intra-city travel. Renewably supplied electricity can deliver long-term, fixed-cost power supply for mobility services throughout the economy, and solar electrons can become a transportation fuel.

From the perspective of energy security and competitive advantage too, new mobility solutions will reduce oil import costs, lower trade deficits, and limit vulnerability to oil supply disruptions and process shocks. Finally, shared, connected and clean-mobility solutions will deliver a host of environmental benefits, including cleaner air so Indian citizens can breathe more easily.

Addressing the Global Mobility Summit, Prime Minister Narendra Modi had outlined a vision for the future of mobility in India based on the seven Cs, which are common, connected, convenient, congestion-free, charged, clean and cutting-edge. How can India achieve these objectives?

First, India's per capita car ownership is quite low with fewer than 20 vehicles per 1,000 persons, as compared to 900 per 1,000 in the US and 800 per 1,000 in Europe. India has an opportunity to leapfrog ahead of the legacy model of individually owned internal combustion engine (ICE) vehicles that are utilized by only around 5 per cent of the people. India's low per capita car ownership affords it the chance to pursue a different model from the Western world. Our emphasis must be on shared, connected and electric transportation.

Second, two- and three-wheelers constitute almost 80 per cent of India's domestic automobile sales. India must leverage this and provide impetus to electrification of these two segments to provide size and scale to India's e-mobility efforts.

Third, India must push for public transportation to become the preferred mode of travel. At present, India has only 1.2 buses per 1,000 people, which is far below the benchmarks of developing nations. Only 63 of the 458 Indian cities have a formal city bus system and 15 cities have a bus or rail-based mass rapid transport system. Public transport must become the core focus area for municipalities and state governments.

Fourth, as we shift from ICE vehicles (2,000 components) to EVs (20 components) India must create a unique ecosystem to encourage and ensure 'Make in India' as far as possible. This would require a phased manufacturing programme across the entire value chain, an efficient fiscal and tax structure, and size and scale aligned to India's ambition to produce world-class vehicles for domestic and global markets. This ecosystem should also be able to attract global original equipment manufacturers for manufacturing.

Fifth, batteries account for almost 40 per cent of the total purchase cost of EVs today. Domestic battery manufacturing is a massive market opportunity for India to rapidly enable the transition to EVs. A recent study by Rocky Mountain Institute and NITI Aayog concludes that India has the opportunity to pursue manufacturing of both battery cells and packs while importing only raw materials. With this, India can capture nearly 80 per cent of the total economic opportunity. New battery technologies, like solid-state lithium-ion batteries, sodium-ion batteries and silicon-based batteries, are under development. India needs to vigorously pursue research and development in these areas and have a clear roadmap for manufacturing on a mega scale.

Lastly, India's cities must build charging infrastructure to remove range anxieties. The existing network of our marketing oil companies must be fully utilized to ensure charging facilities in urban areas and highways.

Forecasts indicate that EVs can reach price parity with ICE vehicles by 2024. India must, therefore, explore newer models of swapping batteries and pay as you go, and facilitate start-ups like Ola, Ather, Sun Mobility, Zoomcar, Shuttl and Rivigo, who are innovating and disrupting status quo in mobility. Our IITs and engineering institutions must also include courses on new technologies as an essential component of their curriculum. States must drive uptake of these solutions by dynamic models of charging a fee for polluting combustion vehicles, while providing rebates on EVs and tightening norms of fuel efficiency across vehicle segments.

A recent report by Morgan Stanley titled 'India's Transport Evolution', has highlighted that on account of rapid spread of digitization, mobile telephony and low per capita car usage, half of India's car fleet will be EVs and half of all miles driven will be on shared platforms by 2040. This new sunrise area can emerge as the biggest catalyst of clean environment, lower trade deficit and new jobs for India.

# Unleashing India's Manufacturing

The Prime Minister's clarion call of 'Make in India' has brought manufacturing centre stage and emphasized its significance in driving India's growth and creating jobs.

A strong, vigorous and dynamic manufacturing sector has to be central to India's economic growth. The future of India's growth process lies in the dynamism of its manufacturing sector. If India has to grow at a rate of 9–10 per cent per annum over the next three decades and create jobs for its young population, the manufacturing sector must grow at 15–16 per cent per annum on a sustained basis. Most of the manufacturing jobs have continued to be in the informal sector, which is characterized by extremely low productivity and poor wages, sans labour laws. The small informal firms in India employ 40 per cent of our workforce as compared to only 4 per cent in Korea and 5.8 per cent in Japan.

While in China, Brazil and South Africa, the manufacturing sector has grown at higher rates than the GDP, in India the share of manufacturing in GDP has stagnated at 16 per cent and accounts for a mere 12 per cent of the workforce. However, manufacturing contributes almost 50 per cent of India's exports and every job created in manufacturing has a multiplier effect, creating three jobs in the services sector.

We are passing through a window of demographic transition that rarely happens in history. We will be adding nearly 138 million to our working age population by 2021–22. This is an astonishing number and manufacturing must catalyze large-scale employment opportunities. Manufacturing in India has been constrained by two critical factors—lack of global size and scale of physical infrastructure, and redundant and outdated labour laws, which have no relevance in today's age and time.

Enhancing the share of manufacturing from 16 per cent to 25 per cent and creating additional employment of 100 million jobs is a national challenge. This implies that the manufacturing sector must grow at rates of 16 per cent per annum on a sustained basis between 2012–13 and 2022–23. We need to not merely create additional employment but arrest the pace of decline in employment intensity in manufacturing. Only if this decline is halved, we would be able to create another 50 million jobs. Almost 70 per cent additional jobs will come from policy measures which will provide impetus to employment intensity. Therefore, employment generation from manufacturing will be a consequence of both manufacturing growth and enhancement in employment intensity. This necessitates skill development on a vast scale and flexible labour laws.

Achieving this will require a single-minded commitment to growth, with emphasis on job-creation rather than job-protection strategies. India will have to radically transform its manufacturing sector by focusing on large-scale labour-intensive factories producing exportable goods, reducing the share of employment in agriculture from the present 58 per cent to 25 per cent by 2030, with industry doubling its labour demand.

The new government has initiated several far-reaching measures to drive manufacturing—it has radically improved the Ease of Doing Business index by business process re-engineering, putting clearances and approvals online and reducing human intervention. It has opened the FDI regime up to 100 per cent in rail, deregulated a vast number of items in defence, and has taken FDI from 26 per cent to 49 per cent—in cases of modernization and state-of-the-art, even up to 100 per cent. It has also vastly liberalized the FDI entry and exit in construction sector. It has also focused on improving the manufacturing infrastructure by focusing on industrial corridors and smart cities.

What more does India need to do to usher in a manufacturing revolution? First, if the sector has to grow in the region of 15–16 per cent over the medium term, exports have to play a critical role and they must accelerate at a much faster pace and achieve growth rates of 25–30 per cent in real terms. Second, SMEs account for 40 per cent of India's workforce and contribute to 45 per cent of India's manufacturing output. SMEs play a significant role in generating millions of jobs. India needs to enhance their scale of operations, ensure better adoption of technology, provide innovative financing and a mechanism for upgrading skills of workers. Third, labour- intensive sectors like food processing apparels and textiles, leather and footwear contribute to over 60 per cent of SMEs' employment. Greater focus on the growth of labour-intensive sectors will enable absorption of the growing surplus of unskilled labour, particularly in UP, Bihar and Jharkhand. Fourth, as energy costs have a major bearing on the manufacturing sector, India needs to quickly get its power sector back on track by removing constraints on coal and gas. Fifth, given that freight and logistics' costs are enormously high and 70 per cent of container transportation is through roads, a modal shift from road to rail is necessary. The Eastern and Western Dedicated Freight Corridors should lead to a radical reduction in freight costs. Sixth, port infrastructure needs a radical overhaul as the average turnaround time in India is 3.5 days as against a mere 10 hours in Hong Kong and 16.5 hours in Colombo. Such lack of world-class physical infrastructure has led to the IMD World Competitiveness Survey, rating India at a lowly 54th among 57 countries in infrastructure facilities.

For large-scale manufacturing to take off, India must be transformed into an attractive investment, defined by easy availability of land, labour and capital. Enforcing contracts in India takes twice the time it takes in OECD (the Organisation for Economic Co-operation and Development) countries and costs almost 40 per cent of the contract signed. India's archaic labour laws are the most rigid in the world. They protect workers not jobs and adversely impact economies of scales and investment. Land and labour laws, therefore, require a drastic overhaul and need to be simplified.

The new government has focused on development of industrial clusters where it can create an ecosystem of supply-chain responsiveness, lower logistic costs, availability of labour and technology upgradation. These clusters will converge the advantages of higher innovation and employment generation for smaller firms with the scale and cost advantage of larger organizations. These advantages are visible in auto-ancillary clusters in Tamil Nadu and pharma-clusters in Andhra Pradesh. The clusters will provide cost and productivity gains and drive India up in the manufacturing chain.

The 'Make in India' initiative has identified 25 sectors where India can be a global champion. India must improve its competitiveness and companies manufacturing in India must become an integrated part of the global supply chains.

Over the next two decades, there will be a huge shift of manufacturing capacity from the developed to the emerging economies. India must capture a disproportionate share of this shift to create jobs for its very young population.

FIVE

# JUDICIARY

# Courts Must Take Into Account the Economic Impact of Their Judgements

The recent order by the Supreme Court of India suspending the Environmental Clearance (EC) of the project and putting a stop to all work for the Mopa Airport development in Goa could gravely harm job creation, travel and tourism, and 'Make in India'. Citing the environment as tantamount to the constitutional right to live, the court has set aside the fact that Goa critically needs a second airport, and that the Environment Assessment Committee (EAC) and National Green Tribunal (NGT) have both held in favour of an EC being granted. This retrospective suspension of the EC is going to startle the investor confidence in India to virtual lockdown status.

The Honourable Court uses the example of SDGs and the new and enhanced threshold of the environmental rule of law for which the court states that the 'benefits of environmental rule of law extend far beyond the environmental sector'. The environment is indeed critical and the court does well to cite the SDGs and their adherence. NITI Aayog is leading the charge when it comes to attaining India's SDGs, and has done cutting-edge work in assessing the issues with water in India through the much-lauded Composite Water Management Index and report. In fact, NITI Aayog recently undertook the extensive exercise of measuring India and its states' progress towards the SDGs for 2030, culminating in the development of the first SDG India Index—Baseline Report 2018—intended to provide a holistic view on the social, economic and environmental status of the country, its states and the UTs.

The court states that the development agenda of the nation must be carried out in compliance with norms stipulated for the protection of the environment and its complexities, that there must be as a balance between development and protection of the environment—there is no trade-off between the two. And yet, it does treat the environment and economic development as binaries. The court acknowledges that the SDGs include the principles of sustainable development and economic growth, but does not provide a means to reconcile them in the context of the Goa Airport. The court does not conduct or order a proper cost-benefit analysis, and by calling into question the expertise, jurisdiction, and to some extent the intent of both the EAC as well as the NGT, it is doing an injustice to the Indian economy.

Tourism is the lifeblood of Goa's economy, and in fact, a major contributor to the Indian economy through employment and revenues. Tourism generates large-scale good-quality employment. It accounts for nearly 40 million jobs in India, with 26 million through direct employment, and 14 million through indirect employment, combining for a massive 9.3 per cent of total employment. The multiplier effects of tourism are immense and if high-quality jobs have to be created, tourism will have to be a key driver of growth.

## THE REAL BALANCE

It is one thing to take into account the ecology, sensitivity and fragility of the environment, but to put a complete stop to a critically important project that will greatly enhance India's most popular tourism destination's capacity is going to irreparably harm 'Make in India,' investor confidence and foreign investment. From the private sector's perspective, nothing will be sacrosanct when it comes to doing business. If despite having received the necessary clearance, having had an expert committee analyse and allow the EC to go through, and having it upheld by a traditionally conservative tribunal that rarely rules in favour of market enterprise as it is, the Supreme Court steps in and retrospectively puts a stop to a key infrastructure project, the Indian economy will suffer, and suffer badly.

What further hurts in this judgement is that the test for assessment has its goalposts consistently shifted, and no business will be able to make the necessary risk assessment to factor in this uncertainty. The greater public good is the norm that the Supreme Court has followed in recent years, but introducing the governance of environmental law as the new threshold and linking it to the right to life under the Indian constitution will make this a barrier to any industry's entry point.

## NGT UPHOLDING THE EC AND PRECEDENTS

The NGT verdict itself was telling, saying it was 'not a case where the project compromises with the environment, as claimed by the appellants.' Then, in the T.N. Godavarman Thirumulpad matter, the court said,

> It cannot be disputed that no development is possible without some adverse effect on the ecology and environment, and the projects of public utility cannot be abandoned and it is necessary to adjust the interest of the people as well as the necessity to maintain the environment. A balance has to be struck between the two interests. Where the commercial venture or enterprise would bring in results which are far more useful for the people, difficulty of a small number of people has to be bypassed. The comparative hardships have to be balanced and the convenience and benefit to a larger section of the people has to get primacy over comparatively lesser hardship.

It would be difficult to make a better argument for the new Goa airport than in the court's own words. The existing Goa airport is widely considered among Asia's worst airports.

## ECONOMIC IMPACT

Add to this the intent of the crucial Shivashakti judgement of Justice A.K. Sikri and Justice A.M. Sapre, where the court observed that the economic impact and effect of a decision ought to be kept in mind, and critically, the court needed to 'avoid that particular outcome which has a potential to create an adverse effect on employment, growth of infrastructure or economy or the revenue of the state.' Similarly, Justice Nariman in the Swiss Ribbons judgement reiterated that the court usually does not substitute its judgement in matters of economic policy and that 'to stay experimentation in things economic is a grave responsibility, and denial of the right to experiment is fraught with serious consequences'.

Unfortunately, these laudable suggestions appear to not have been implemented in some of the recent judgments, especially the Goa Airport one. In fact, this is the second crippling decision taken by the Honourable Supreme Court with regard to the state of Goa, following close on the heels of the Goa Foundation matter, where the court cancelled renewals of all iron ore mining leases in Goa.

For a state entirely dependent on iron ore production and tourism for revenue, the cost to the economy exceeds hundreds of crore in lost revenue. Even the court took cognizance of the impact to the economy in the Goa Foundation matter, when borrowing from the Grant of Mining Leases Policy that placed the loss of foreign exchange through exports at approximately $8 billion, upwards of ₹850 crore towards loans/advances on the mining sector for a variety of activities as well as approximately ₹1000 crore towards housing, business and other loans. The court further noted that there was a slump in economic activity that extended to the education sector and others. This is extremely unfortunate and devastating to the people of Goa.

## ECONOMIC COST OF THE RULING

In the current matter, there have been significant costs to conducting business, and there have been major outflows which will be adversely impacted by this judgement. The indicative capital for Phase I of the development is ₹1,900 crore while the cost of the entire project is likely to be ₹3,000 crore. The state of Goa has incurred a total expenditure of ₹240 crore for land acquisition, rehabilitation, road widening, consultancy and other related aspects while the concessionaire has already incurred an expenditure of ₹230 crore. Around 14 per cent of the project work has been completed and a manpower consisting of 2,000 persons has been mobilized at the site together with plant and machinery. All of this has come to a halting stop.

And this happened when the court has been intimated that the need for a new airport is critical. There is no doubt that Goa needs to significantly expand capacity for flights. In fact, the expected inflow of passengers is anticipated to reach 30 million in 2030.

## CONCLUSION

Fittingly, the Supreme Court has in the past ordered that policy decisions should not be open to judicial review if they pass the test of reasonableness. A bench comprising of present Chief Justice of India (CJI) Ranjan Gogoi and Justice Ashok Bhushan in Union of India vs. M Selvakumar in 2017 held that there was nothing arbitrary in the decision taken by the centre and the high courts should not have interfered with it.

The Goa Airport matter is another example of the increasing uncertainty and cost of doing business in India due to interventions by the judiciary after statutory approvals. It's a dangerous precedent to set, and ironical when seen in the context of judgements like Shivashakti. The environment is vitally important, and so is development. It is time for the fine balance that is so often mentioned in orders by the court to actually play out in ground realities.

# Justice Has Been Served but the Supreme Court Judgement on Aadhaar Should Have Gone Further to Enhance Efficiency Through Technology

The Supreme Court judgement affirming the constitutionality and importance of Aadhaar validates the Government of India's effort at promoting good governance and ensuring that the maximum benefit extends to those who need it the most. It is also a validation of the magnitude of the initiative which has greatly reduced leakages in disbursements, and brought an element of clockwork precision to enhancing efficiency of time and resources. Over ₹90,000 crore is saved every year by plugging leakages in over 500 welfare schemes through the usage of Aadhaar for authentication.

However, in limiting the scope of the use of Aadhaar for validation by the private sector, the judgement has not gone far enough. Technology has streamlined every process, especially through the use of Aadhaar and biometrics for authentication.

The process of opening a bank account, applying for a loan, taking out an insurance policy, or even using Aadhaar-enabled payment systems has reduced the red-tape, paperwork, time spent, and therefore economic efficiency of all these processes. What would take months and years prior to the Aadhaar-enabling, now takes minutes if not seconds. It has also ensured that a much larger number of individuals can benefit from the efficiency, since technology ensures that the far reaches of the previously unreachable areas can now avail the benefits of authenticating through their Aadhaar and corresponding services.

By striking down Section 57 of the Aadhaar Act which allows private entities to use the process, the Supreme Court unfortunately has done the ease of doing business a great disservice. The customer acquisition costs had been reduced by nearly 90 per cent, and as mentioned earlier, mutually beneficial outcomes through Aadhaar-enabling had benefited both the residents of India as well as private sector entities. What the court merely should have done is allowed Section 57 to stand, and directed the government to create a strong legal framework that would set out the terms of use, and protect the privacy of individuals who provided their Aadhaar details for authentication purposes. Privacy cannot and should not be linked directly to Aadhaar-enabling. There should only be a law that protects privacy and therefore regulates data usage and acquisition. In this, the court should have not interfered since the economic outcomes from judgements must also be taken into consideration given how many hundreds of millions of people have benefitted from the technological efficiency and advancement brought in by Aadhaar-enabling.

It is important to recognize that the business use for Aadhaar enabling or authenticating is critical for the ease of doing business and for maximizing technology enhanced economic efficiency. Yes, a critical aspect of the Aadhaar is as a social welfare mobilizer, and also as a necessary form of identity for one and all. Having said that, the Aadhaar has an enormous role to play in achieving a cashless, transparent, efficient and an inclusive economy and ecosystem. E-KYC and Aadhaar-enabled validation has been a game changer for many sectors, and boosted capability and capacity. To roll that back as per the judgement would cause irreparable paralysis to efficiency and capacity and adversely impact productivity in the Indian economy.

Some of the major benefits of the Aadhaar that cut across socio-economic lines were the ease of meeting address proof requirements, and the ease with which businesses could conduct authentication for a myriad services irrespective of geographical location or demographic position. Getting a SIM card, a basic health or vehicle insurance plan or opening a bank account, to name a few services, all require address proof. The Aadhaar was the address proof requirement that made everyone's life significantly easier on both sides of the coin. For the service receiver, it removed difficult layers of requirements for an acceptable form of address proof, and for the service provider, it eliminated reams of paperwork and associated costs that go with the red tape, to ensure that customer service was economical and efficient merely through biometrics and an Aadhaar number. All of this now appears to be in disarray because of the unnecessary component of the ruling. And all of this could merely have been tackled by retaining it and issuing a directive for the enabling and protection of the law. Many sectors will be impacted by this judgement. Banks, who were utilizing e-KYC measures, will now face time lags and costs the insurance sector, which was able to have online authentication of customers leading to quick and seamless issuance of policies; and other aspects such as reducing fraud and impersonation. Now, verification will not merely be slower but costlier.

An even more worrying prospect could also loom. With the uncertainty caused by the rollback of the provision for private sector entities, the entities may now be wary of using biometrics and Aadhaar authentication processes going forward. This would be a devastating outcome and undo the years of effort spent to enhance speed, accountability and efficiency. This is why something must be done at the earliest to clarify the way forward.

Make no mistake—this is a landmark ruling that reposes the utmost and complete faith in the Aadhaar by the Supreme Court. And, the majority ruling also ensures that the untiring efforts by the Government of India to ensure that the benefits in the social sectors reach the intended beneficiaries will continue and have been validated. Also validated is the need to bring transparency in income tax filings and related objectives. However, the economic impact of this ruling could be significantly costly and bring back inefficiency. This is why a law that ensures privacy while removing barriers to unrelated and necessary activities are allowed within a proper legal framework will have to be the likely next step. What could also be considered is the usage of a public blockchain for enhancing security, transparency and privacy. Transparency and good governance will continue to prevail through this judgement, and so must the ease of doing business for the benefit of each and every resident of India. The eventual goal must be to empower and institutionalize efficiency-advance governance by adopting technology and, at the same time, to make sure that it is economically sound.

# How to Speed Up Judiciary: Let's Make India's Slow Courts, Currently Exacting an Enormous Human and Economic Toll, World-Class

The facts that the order for the arrest of Justice Karnan as well as the extremely high-profile Nirbhaya case took more than four years to resolve are pointers of India's larger judicial crisis. About three crore cases are currently pending in various courts of India. According to an analysis, if the nation's judges closed 100 cases every hour without eating or sleeping, it would take more than 35 years to catch up. Fifty-seven per cent of district and subordinate court cases take more than 10 years to dispose of.

India ranks 178th among 189 countries on the enforcing contracts indicator, making it one of India's worst performing indicators in World Bank's Ease of Doing Business index study. This largely accounts for India's overall poor ranking and has acted as a major barrier for investments to India.

Ex-CJI Khehar's call for judges to give up five days of their summer vacation for the sake of the nation could not have been timelier. In fact, one wonders why the judiciary has a summer vacation at all.

The glut of cases in the lower courts is where the root of the problem lie. Most importantly, we need to acknowledge it and monitor it on a continuing basis. We need to have access to high-resolution data on judicial processes at both the high court as well as the lower court level. A number of courts do not have data under the 'date filed' column, the most crucial piece for identifying delays.

The quality of data is circumspect and is non-uniform between courts, which use different abbreviations, categorization and formats which makes comparing data between courts an arduous and costly process. Significant progress has been made towards computerization of courts. However, computerization must include within its ambit the standardization of data collection across courts and not merely computerization within silos.

The Allahabad High Court has an average of 77 hearings per judge per day whereas Calcutta High Court does 148 hearings. No judge-specific metrics are available. If we even had simple metrics like the frequency of case disposal per judge or categorization of subject matter with respect to judges, a great deal of accountability and trust would be brought into the system.

The collegium would have more data points to objectively decide on elevation of judges. The CJI's office and high courts should have a live dashboard which can update them on the performance of the high courts, justices, and the aggregated data of the lower courts, with simple colour-coded markers for various key performance indicators.

New technology should be leveraged and not just technology for data collection. AI is fast maturing, and with further advances in machine learning, standardized data collection can assist judges in forming judgements. A software developed by Nine Research Institute in China helped 300 judges handle 1,50,000 cases, reducing their workload by a third.

Today, civil society is increasingly inclined to blame judges alone for delays. This is unfair. The office of a judge of the Delhi High Court was barricaded by lawyers because he imposed costs on flippant requests for adjournment! Lawyers, who charge per appearance, have a vested interest in getting repeated adjournments so that cases can drag on further. Video conferencing is statutorily provided but rarely available in practice and infrequently used even if available. Accountability needs to be fixed on individuals, causing repeated delays in dispensing justice.

The time taken for the disposal of cases is also widely divergent across different categories of cases. According to a report by DAKSH, the number of steps required to decide a civil revision petition are not fewer than those needed for civil or criminal appeals. However, civil revision petitions are decided on average in 77 days at Bombay High Court whereas civil appeals take 2,303 days on an average. This suggests that case management in procedure law in India needs to be overhauled.

'Case management hearings' that should be introduced after pleadings have been completed by both parties where timelines are set and the court should impose sanctions against parties that fail to adhere to these timelines. Also, we should have a consolidated 'adjournment manual' applicable across all courts which codifies the conditions under which adjournment should be granted in order to reduce arbitrariness.

Economic uncertainty in decision-making is further compounded by periodic encroachment by the judiciary in the domain of the executive. Two recent examples are the high court of Tamil Nadu asking the state government to waive farmers' loans and the highway liquor ban imposed by the Supreme Court. The short-term perspective furthered by these encroachments is severely impacting long-term predictability, consistency and clarity of policies. In several cases, they involve livelihood losses for citizens who are not even a party to the case.

To substantially de-risk investments into India, we need to quickly operationalize commercial courts in Delhi and Mumbai as a first step and update the rules of procedure for commercial cases to reduce the backlog of these cases and to improve India's rank in the Doing Business report of the World Bank.

The high pendency in courts can decline only with effective measurement, process overhaul, constant feedback, and by equipping the judiciary with technology and modern tools. This alone can enable the emergence of a new and modern judicial system with the capacity to dispense justice speedily—for, as we all know, justice delayed is justice denied.

# No More 'Tareek Pe Tareek': Stop Adjourning Justice

'No more "tareek pe tareek". No more adjournments. Enough is enough', ordered Justice Gautam Patel of Mumbai High Court in a recent judgement. He added, 'That a court will endlessly grant adjournments is not something that parties or advocates can take for granted. Nor should they assume that there will be no more consequences to continued defaults and unexpected delay.'

The National Judicial Data Grid estimates that there are approximately 2.6 crore cases pending, with approximately 65 lakh cases pending for over five years. A study has stated that it takes almost 20 years for a property-related dispute to be resolved, and if the rate of disposal continues and there are no new cases, it will take 324 years to clear the present backlog. According to former CJI Mr M.N. Venkatachaliah, the 'loss of man hours, wages and productivity is estimated at ₹50,387 crore per year, in addition to the actual wasted expenses of ₹30,000 crore per year!' The contribution of excessive adjournments to the delay in disposal of cases in India is a critical aspect that has been recognized repeatedly by the Supreme Court of India. It has repeatedly stressed that adjournments dent the efficacy of judicial process, and if not curtailed effectively, it will lead to public losing faith in the judicial process.

Another former CJI Dipak Misra had, in a petition in 2011, asked the judiciary 'to conceive and adopt a mechanism, regard being had to the priority of cases, to avoid such inordinate delays in matters.' In another matter, Justice Misra, on the plight of the plaintiff, a septuagenarian, observed how despite 'the difficulties faced by an old man when he is compelled to come to court so many times' to give evidence, the trial court still adjourned the matter, further stating, 'The virus of seeking adjournment has to be controlled. The saying of Gita "Awake! Arise! Oh Partha" is apt here to be stated for guidance of trial courts.'

It's clear from the Supreme Court's observations that unfettered delays continue to inconvenience those seeking justice. Only 10 per cent of subordinate cases make it to the high court, and of the high court cases, only 2 per cent make it to Supreme Court. Majority of the cases are in lower courts where the root of the problem lies. It is here that the issue of adjournments impact the public and has to be tackled. The legislature has, through an amendment in 1999, fixed an upper limit of three adjournments during the hearing of a matter. It specifically disallows the courts from expanding the time granted for doing any 'act prescribed or allowed by the code' beyond a maximum period of 30 days. This was reiterated in 2002 when, another time frame to prevent delays was introduced, limiting the time for filing written statements to 90 days from the date of service of summons.

However, despite the statutory procedure built into the system, the interpretation of two infamous Supreme

Court judgements of 2005, namely, the Salem Advocate Bar Association case and the Kailash vs Nanhku matter, has inadvertently created loopholes allowing delays through excessive adjournments in the interest of providing justice.

In the Salem Advocate Bar Association case, the Supreme Court interpreted the limitation of time frame of 30 days as one not attenuating the inherent power of Indian courts to 'pass orders as may be necessary for the ends of justice or to prevent abuse of process of the court.' And in the Kailash vs Nanhku matter, the Supreme Court again relaxed the statutorily prescribed deadline for the filing of written statements by interpreting them as 'merely directive and not mandatory.' Bolstered by these two judgements, lawyers have had a free hand to routinely file written statements beyond 90 days. And in a baffling outcome, the courts have continued to assert their inherent right to endlessly adjourn to justify their 'sense of justice.'

Delays and pendency have been addressed recently in two extremely timely publications that help broaden the discourse. The Economic Survey 2018, in its section on timely justice, stresses that building additional capacity of the judiciary may not be effective unless existing capacity is fully utilized, estimating that the higher judiciary is currently operating at only 63.6 per cent of existing capacity. It points out that enough has been done to ease business and commerce but the next step is to address pendency, delays and backlogs in the judicial arena. Equally significant is the Ease of Doing Business Report 2018 (EoDB Report) which highlights how non-enforcement of the legal procedure for grant of adjournments by the judiciary is responsible for these delays.

The EoDB Report also observes via its Judicial Processes

Index (JPI) on enforcing contracts that the issue of adjournments is not due to the absence of any legal cap on the number of adjournments that can be granted. The survey meanwhile highlights the role that increasing injunctions by courts play. The JPI, on the other, hand pinpoints how despite having relevant laws to regulate the maximum number of adjournments that can be granted, in India, these are not always implemented.

There's more. A number of studies over the years further affirm that adjournments are one of the key causes for judicial delay. As early as in 1978, the 77th Law Commission Report identified adjournments as an important cause of delay. A report by the National Institute of Public Finance and Policy in 2016 statistically proved that by identifying that, the borrowers seeking adjournments cause 46 per cent of all delays in Debt Recovery Tribunals.

That's not all. Instances of a court easing the stipulated and statutory procedure may be found for nearly every provision in the Code of Civil Procedure that contains a time limit. A recent study of the Delhi High Court by the Vidhi Centre for Legal Policy shows that lawyers asked for adjournments in 97 per cent of cases in the sample collected. Vidhi further found that though courts stress consistently on cost imposition for excessive adjournments, only 20 per cent of the aforementioned delayed cases received any penalty. Another recent study by DAKSH has estimated that subordinate courts in Delhi and Bengaluru spend about 44 per cent of their time and approximately ₹80–150 crore (which is around 12–22 per cent of state annual expenditure on judiciary) on adjournments.

The Supreme Court itself recognizes that unnecessary delays caused by adjournments or of lawyers gaming the system will adversely impact the faith of the common man in the judicial system. The CJI in his presidential address at the 125th anniversary celebration of the Madras High Court building called the practice of 'seeking' adjournments a disease and stated that lawyers 'should develop a sense of anti-allergenic towards adjournments'.

The way forward is clear. There needs to be a new culture, together with zero tolerance for adjournments. Simply put, adjournments should not be granted, and even where granted, every adjournment must bring with it a penalty. And in any circumstance, no adjournments should be granted beyond the statutory limit of three adjournments. There must be no more 'tareek pe tareek' and the policy of zero tolerance for adjournments needs to be mobilized immediately. That is the only way forward.

# Acknowledgements

This publication is a result of several years of service across myriad areas and projects. Along the way, I have worked with several outstanding colleagues in the state of Kerala, DIPP, NITI Aayog, DMIDC and many others. I thank each and every one of them for the hard work they have put into making India a world leading nation.

This book is based to a large extent on articles that have appeared in leading publications. I would like to thank *The Times of India*, *Economic Times*, *Hindustan Times*, *Livemint*, and *Open* magazine in which several of the articles of this book were first published.

I would also like to acknowledge the contribution of my good friends Param Iyer and Indu Bhushan for each co-authoring an article with me, which has been carried in this book.

I appreciate the inputs of Sujeet Samaddar on some of the essays that are a part of this collection.

I thank Desh Gaurav Sekhri for his continued support in this endeavor.

Finally, I am grateful to the entire Team Rupa for publishing this book.

derived from speeches that I have delivered in the past couple of years, and that have not been published earlier. These are:

a. Address at the 40th Directors Conference of DRDO, 29 December 2017 (Adapted as *DRDO's Tremendous Potential to Spearhead Our Transformation to a New India)*
b. Address at the Naval Commanders Conference 2017: 24 October 2017 (Adapted as '*The Unlimited Potential for the Navy to Reinvent Itself and Become an Integral Part of the New India Revolution*')
c. Address at the International Foundation for Aviation, Aerospace and Drones Conference on 17th July 2019 (Adapted as *'NewSpace Technologies for a Transformational New India')*
d. Address at FICCI's 'Make in India for Unmanned Aircraft Systems—Promoting UAS Industry in India' Conference, 11 July 2018 (Adapted as *'The Limitless Potential for Unmanned Aircraft Systems industry to Soar in New India'*)